The Real Hergé

For Dorrie and Joan

The Real Hergé

The Inspiration Behind Tintin

Sian Lye

WHITE OWL

AN IMPRINT OF PEN & SWORD BOOKS LTD.
YORKSHIRE – PHILADELPHIA

First published in Great Britain in 2020 by
White Owl
An imprint of
Pen & Sword Books Ltd
Yorkshire – Philadelphia

Copyright © Sian Lye 2020

ISBN 978 1 52676 390 7

The right of Sian Lye to be identified as Author of this work has been
asserted by her in accordance with the Copyright, Designs and Patents
Act 1988.

A CIP catalogue record for this book is
available from the British Library.

Typeset by Mac Style
Printed and bound in the UK by TJ Books Limited,
Padstow, Cornwall.

MIX
Paper from
responsible sources
FSC® C013056

Pen & Sword Books Limited incorporates the imprints of Atlas,
Archaeology, Aviation, Discovery, Family History, Fiction, History,
Maritime, Military, Military Classics, Politics, Select, Transport,
True Crime, Air World, Frontline Publishing, Leo Cooper, Remember
When, Seaforth Publishing, The Praetorian Press, Wharncliffe
Local History, Wharncliffe Transport, Wharncliffe True Crime
and White Owl.

For a complete list of Pen & Sword titles please contact

PEN & SWORD BOOKS LIMITED
47 Church Street, Barnsley, South Yorkshire, S70 2AS, England
E-mail: enquiries@pen-and-sword.co.uk
Website: www.pen-and-sword.co.uk

Or

PEN AND SWORD BOOKS
1950 Lawrence Rd, Havertown, PA 19083, USA
E-mail: Uspen-and-sword@casematepublishers.com
Website: www.penandswordbooks.com

Contents

Acknowledgements

With thanks to Kate Bohdanowicz, Michelle Higgs, Gavan Curley, Justine Hawkins, Sam Lye, Peter Lye, Jim Lewis and all at Pen & Sword Books.

Introduction

Hergé, otherwise known as Georges Prosper Remi, is one of the best-loved authors in history, yet also one of the most controversial. He created only twenty-four Tintin books, but *The Adventures of Tintin* have sold more than 250 million copies worldwide in an eventful career, have been translated into more than 110 languages and are considered to be one of the greatest comic series of all time.

Now, thirty-seven years after his death, Hergé remains an enigma and a phenomenon. He survived a barrage of scandals, including accusations of racism and anti-Semitism. He was also attacked for appearing to collaborate with the Nazis during the Second World War.

His personal life was no easier. Although he had a loving mother, she suffered from mental health issues and would end up in a psychiatric hospital. In his later years, he would hint at surviving abuse from a relative and would also mention the abuse that was rife within his former Scouting troop.

For decades, critics have attacked Hergé's work for racism and sexism, and indeed his original stories do feature racially offensive caricatures considered wholly unacceptable by today's standards.

But Hergé was a product of a different time and reflected the prevailing attitudes of the day. One of his greatest strengths, but also one of his greatest weaknesses, was that he was very easily influenced by a variety of charismatic characters. In many ways this ability to absorb the opinions and talents of others led to some of his best work, but it also led to him making poor political decisions that would continue to haunt him throughout his life.

The criticism he faced greatly affected Hergé: though he would rarely retaliate, he did change aspects of his books to make them more palatable in later years. Indeed, Hergé was an exacting artist who expected the best from others as well as himself. He would often revise previous work before it was to be reprinted, amending anything he felt he could improve, but his perfectionism would cause him no end of health issues.

Ahead of his time, Hergé introduced Europe to the American style of cartoon strip which incorporated speech bubbles and captured the imagination of millions of children and adults alike. Although he was not a gregarious person and was reluctant to attend book signing sessions, he was fiercely loyal to his fans and would write long personal letters in reply, even going so far as to loan money to some of his fans when asked.

Privately, he battled a debilitating depression, and was unhappy with his achievements. Later in life he would say that he hated Tintin, and would have much preferred to have been an artist in the more traditional sense.

Hergé had numerous affairs and wanted to leave his marriage, but felt riddled with guilt from his Catholic upbringing and Boy Scout ethos. He was unable to have children and did not want to have a family in any case as they would have disturbed his work too much; he had a great need for peace and quiet. His friends would say he didn't have the knack for happiness.

Always searching for more, Hergé was interested in new ideas and new people. He loved jazz music, and by the 1950s, his latest passion was Pop Art and the modern abstract styles. The paranormal always held a fascination for him, and in later life he would rely on the opinion of a clairvoyant. While going through a particularly tumultuous period, he recorded his traumatic dreams and consulted a Jungian psychoanalyst for help. After meeting Zhang Chongren in the 1930s, he carried a lifelong interest in Eastern philosophy, particularly the writings of the Tao.

He was a complex and naive man in many ways, haunted by the demons of his past and desperate to escape the work he had been so successful in. His constant need to run away frustrated those who worked with him, and he lacked the courage of the famous hero he created. In many ways, he remained a lost little boy scout who never really grew up. But his artwork and meticulous plotting were exceptional and paved the way for graphic comics. Hergé has left a canon of work that children and adults the world over continue to love.

Chapter 1

In the spring of 1907, Alexis Remi and his wife Elisabeth welcomed their first child, a son they named Georges Prosper Remi. In typical reserved fashion, Alexis was not there at the birth and the doctor had to sign the birth certificate. The couple had just bought their first house together – a modest family home in Etterbeek, a peaceful suburb of Brussels. They hoped for a quiet, stable career for Georges, possibly in the army, and never dreamed he would achieve global success as an artist.

Alexis and his twin Léon were born in 1882 to Marie Léonie Dewigne, an unmarried 22-year-old, who worked for the Countess Helene Erremault de Dudzeele as a chambermaid. The countess let the mother and boys live on the family estate of Chaumont-Gistoux in Brabant, near Brussels, alongside the two daughters of the house, Germaine and Valentine, with the countess educating them as if they were her own. She would dress them in beautiful clothes and often take the twins on a carriage ride into the town for a treat. The twins were even able to attend school until they were 14 years old, which was a rarity at the time.

However, when the twins were 14, the countess unceremoniously gave the family their marching orders, and they moved out into the lower middle classes.

In September 1893, Marie married her cousin, a significantly younger man, Philippe Remi, who was 23 at the time and worked as a printer. He gave the family its surname. Although it seemed the young man had simply volunteered to give the family an air of respectability, he and Marie continued to live together until her death in 1901. After her death, little is known of Philippe. He signed the marriage certificate of Alexis Remi as 'father', but never met Hergé and died in 1941.

It was generally assumed that the biological father of the twins was someone from the chateau, possibly the master of the house, Count Gaston Errembault de Dudzeele. However, one frequent visitor to Chaumont-Gistoux was Belgium's then king, Leopold II, and it is a Belgian legend that Leopold is Hergé's ancestor.

Later in life, Georges would often casually mention to colleagues that his family came from Chaumont-Gistoux, without giving any further details, rather enjoying the mystery that surrounded him.

With a childhood enveloped in luxury, the move was difficult for Alexis, who found himself working for the clothing manufacturer Demoulin at the age of 14, making clothes for young people. Eventually he became a well-respected worker and often worked directly with the boss, Henri Van Roye-Waucquez, who was impressed with Hergé's father partly because he came from such a supposedly affluent background.

In 1905, at the age of 23, Alexis married his childhood sweetheart, Elisabeth. She was from the Marolles quarter of Brussels, born in the same year as her husband, 1882. She worked as a seamstress, but gave up work when she married.

Alexis and Elisabeth set up home close to Elisabeth's parents on 25 de la rue Cranz in Etterbeek, and they lived a quiet life in the reserved Roman Catholic suburb, where Georges Prosper Remi was born at 7.30 am on 22 May 1907. One year later, the family moved to 34 rue de Theux and it was here that Georges spent his childhood.

Elisabeth constantly struggled with health problems. Before Georges was born, she nearly died from pleurisy, and towards the end of 1909, she had a major relapse. Alexis thought she had passed away and searched anxiously for a priest, but she pulled through and he would forever proclaim the incident was a miracle.

However, she remained in frail health, often sick and would suffer blackouts too, which was especially difficult for the family as Alexis would have to travel for work; he would often be away for long periods at a time, sending home long, loving letters to the wife he doted on, urging her to have courage and patience.

Elisabeth was a loving mother to Georges in the early years and he was very close to her. He didn't go to kindergarten, preferring to stay with his mother, and she would take him to the cinema each and every week. He would sit in her lap and absorb the work of the pioneers of cinema at the time – Georges Méliès, Max Linder and Buster Keaton – people who would shape his ideas and creations later on.

Georges' mother also made all his clothes. It was fairly clear she had wanted a girl, as until Georges was 5 years old, he wore dresses and his hair was styled in shoulder-length curls. Elisabeth would carry on making Georges' clothes for most of her life.

Georges loved to draw, even from a very early age, and his parents used to foist pen and paper on the young boy to keep him calm as he would often get into trouble when bored.

In January 1912, the Remis moved again, this time just a few streets away. Two months later, their son Paul arrived and completed their family of four. For Georges, this was a major disruption as he had enjoyed being an adored only child for five years, and Elisabeth was even more indulgent with her second son.

The two boys had completely different personalities and temperaments. Paul was an active, popular boy with a quiff and a round face, while Georges was also outgoing but quieter and more introspective than his brother. Although Paul was a muse for the young artist, the pair were not close growing up.

The Remis were a quiet, undemonstrative family, and while Georges had a close relationship with his mother in the early years, his bond with his father grew stronger as he got older. They would sit and draw together – sometimes his father would teach him how to draw clothes, other times they would while the hours away sketching aeroplanes together, with Georges realising how similar they were, but also how different. While his father would draw his aeroplanes to be as light as insects, his own were brimming with accuracy and engineering.

His father was a curious character, and would often meet with his twin brother, Léon, who lived nearby, to go for long walks together around the neighbourhood singing loudly in unison. With their moustaches, suits and identical bowler hats and canes, they were a clear inspiration for the comical twins Thomson and Thompson in the Tintin books.

The twins were so alike that Georges' mother, Elisabeth, was known to interrogate the two in the evening to make sure she didn't accidentally retire to bed with the wrong brother. Georges remained close to his father, who acted as his business manager and was involved in his work for the rest of his life.

As a young boy, Georges developed a passion for film, having been influenced by the trips to the cinema he had enjoyed as an infant with his mother. He loved an early animation called *Gertie the Dinosaur*, as well as the slapstick work of Buster Keaton and Charlie Chaplin, which his comics would later reference.

Although not a keen bookworm in childhood, Georges did enjoy burrowing himself away in adventure novels such as *Huckleberry Finn*, *Treasure Island* and *Robinson Crusoe*, as well as grittier books by Charles Dickens and Alexandre Dumas.

Georges started at the preparatory school at l'Athénée d'Ixelles in 1913, which was a private, secular school. This was an interesting choice as there were many schools closer to the Remis, and they were unusual in not choosing a Catholic school for their young son. Alexis would occasionally attend Mass, while Elisabeth was less invested in the religion and would only attend Mass very rarely.

Georges was a conscientious student and achieved good grades. He had many friends and enjoyed days full of quiet family life, school and friends. However, in 1914, life was darkened by the death of his grandfather, Elisabeth's father, and the rest of the world was about to be turned upside down.

Soon after Georges' grandfather died, Archduke Franz Ferdinand of Austria, heir presumptive to the throne, and his wife Sophie were assassinated on 28 June, setting into motion a string of events that would alter world history and life in Belgium irreparably.

When the First World War began, Germany invaded Belgium and Luxembourg, both neutral countries, as part of the Schlieffen Plan. The intention was to catch the French off guard with a surprise entry through the neutral countries and capture Paris very quickly.

Britain was bound by an agreement from 1839 to protect Belgium should the country become embroiled in a war, and it was this act that spurred the British to enter the battle.

On 2 August 1914, the German government demanded that German armies be given free passage through Belgian territory, which was refused by the Belgian government the very next day.

The Belgian King, Albert I, addressed his Parliament on 4 August, with a hopeful speech, but one that revealed his deep concern. He said, 'Never since 1830 has a graver hour sounded for Belgium. The strength of our right and the need of Europe for our autonomous existence make us still hope that the dreaded events will not occur.'

That day, German troops were given the signal to invade Belgium. They started at dawn, attacking Liège, which was captured three days later. Groups of resistance fighters formed quickly in Belgium and battled the invading army, but were dealt with brutally by the Germans. The resistance fighters demolished bridges and railway tracks, and the German troops treated any type of resistance as illegal and subversive. They would retaliate by burning buildings and shooting the parties involved.

For Georges, this was the beginning of an extremely tumultuous time. The family was ripped apart when his uncle Léon was sent to war, and he would not be seen again until it was all over.

The effects of the war devastated the country. Thousands of civilians were killed in altercations with the German army as they tore through the country. The population collectively panicked, and the Belgian government fled to France.

On 20 August, the German army invaded Brussels, with a small group of soldiers remaining to protect King Albert. The Germans acted swiftly and soon occupied and governed over 95 per cent of the country, with only the small area around Ypres staying under Belgian control.

Many civilians fled the war zones to safer parts of Belgium. The impact of the war affected Georges' family significantly, and the health of his mother, Elisabeth, rapidly declined. The doctor advised a move to the country, which the family dutifully carried out, leaving for the quieter area of Watermael-Boitsfort. However, it was only a few months before they would return home to their old neighbourhood.

Many other Belgians escaped to the neutral Netherlands and around 300,000 people fled to France, while over 200,000 went to Britain. Here, many people settled in London and worked for the war effort. The governments of Britain and France created the War Refugees Committee (WRC) and the Secours National to help the Belgian refugees.

In 1915, the German authorities built the 'Wire of Death', a lethal electric fence along the Belgian-Dutch border to deter Belgians from escaping. This brutal fence would kill between 2,000 and 3,000 Belgian refugees trying to flee the country.

Although the Belgian government was in exile in France, it instructed the civil servants to stay in their roles and continue their duties during the Occupation, although Parliament was shut down. Many businesses and universities followed suit and closed their doors, while coal miners and farmers continued to work.

A lack of effort was considered to be 'passive resistance' and the Germans would send in managers to operate factories that were underperforming. They also deported able Belgian workers to Germany for forced labour jobs – around 120,000 people were deported by 1918.

Georges left his previous school for Ixelles Municipal School Number 3, which was a free school, as his family could no longer afford to send him to a fee-paying establishment. Indeed, the whole country was struggling at this time with disruption in industries, and a significant lack of food. Georges' neighbourhood of Etterbeek was surrounded by the German military barracks, and so German soldiers were a common sight. It was a difficult and fearful time for the family, and for the rest of Belgian society. The Germans acted brutally, and the soldiers' mistreatment of civilians during this time is often referred to as the 'Rape of Belgium'.

The German army was angry at how the Belgians had fought back during the Schlieffen Plan to capture Paris, and there were rumours within the camp that Belgian civilians had tortured and maltreated German soldiers.

The Germans replied violently to this by destroying a series of historic buildings, as well as orchestrating large-scale attacks, executing around 6,000 French and Belgian civilians between August and November 1914, in random shootings of groups of people, which had been ordered by junior German officers. Anyone suspected of any activity that would derail the German war effort was summarily shot, and high-profile Belgian figures, such as politicians and historians were imprisoned in Germany as hostages. It was a fearful time for the country, marked by brutality and uncertainty.

The Remis moved home a few times during this period, no doubt trying to find the safest place to shield their family, and in 1917 they moved again, this time back to 34 rue de Theux, Elisabeth's family home. The Remis bought out the other siblings' shares of the property and moved in. They allowed the other siblings, as well as Elisabeth's mother, Antoinette, to continue to stay at the house, which was surrounded by fields and countryside. They felt the safest option was for the whole family to stay together, given the situation.

The Remis lived here with Antoinette and other members of the family, including Georges' uncle, Charles Arthur, whose nickname was Tchake. Charles was Elisabeth's younger brother and ten years older than Georges.

The author Benoit Peeters alleges it was at this point that Georges was the victim of sexual abuse by Charles. The rumours arise from unnamed family sources and hints from letters, such as the one that Georges would later write to his secretary, Marcel Dehaye, during one of his depressive episodes. He would write vaguely and indirectly about his childhood and disturbing images that were forever etched into his mind.

The truth of this will certainly remain forever hidden, as this is not something that Georges would later talk about in depth. As with many other personal matters, he would keep anything painful very much to himself and a few close friends.

Whatever the truth, Georges' childhood was not an overly happy time for him, but on the surface, he was like most children, and would spend hours playing outside with his friends and his younger brother; despite the war and family troubles, life went on. When the weather wouldn't allow him to roam the streets and fields, he would hole up inside using his vivid imagination to conjure up adventure stories and illustrate them with detailed sketches.

He loved nothing more than spending quiet hours drawing the new machines of the time such as trains, cars and planes in intricate detail, distracting himself from the brutality of war and a rather distant, aloof family.

When 1918 came around, the First World War ended and left Belgium and the rest of Europe relieved, but in ruins. The priority now was to repair the ravaged country and get back to life as usual.

Georges was nearly 12, and his parents began to think about secondary schools for their eldest boy, and so in 1919, secondary education began for the restless artist at the Place de Londres, a secular school in Ixelles. Here, he continued to hone his artistic skills, sketching out scenes along the edges of his school books.

However, he did not thrive in the new school and his grades suffered, so much so that it was suggested that he should leave to become an apprentice alongside his father, but he stayed and persevered at the school.

One of the reasons for his poor grades during this period was that this was the time the young Georges discovered a pastime that would have a lasting effect on his life – Scouting. He joined the Belgian Boy Scouts while the worldwide organisation was still very much an emerging phenomenon. The group wholly captured the imagination of the young boy and many more like him.

Scouting began just eleven years earlier in the UK, after the 1908 publication of *Scouting for Boys* written by Robert Baden-Powell. Baden-Powell had always loved the outdoors, but it wasn't until the 1880s when he was a military officer stationed in British India that he took an interest in military scouting, and in 1891 he published *Reconnaissance and Scouting*.

In 1899 Baden-Powell was in South Africa during the Second Boer War, and found himself besieged in the small town of Mafeking by a much larger Boer army. Here Baden-Powell became aware of the Mafeking Cadet Corps – a group of youths that supported the troops by carrying messages, which freed the men for military duties and kept the boys occupied during the long siege. He found the group incredibly inspiring.

Meanwhile, Baden-Powell was becoming a celebrity back in the UK, as newspapers reported heavily on the siege and a rapt public followed the army's every move. When the siege was broken Baden-Powell returned to the country a national hero.

The youths who had helped the troops had so impressed Baden-Powell that he was motivated to tell others about the skills they had used. He wrote another book – this time a small instruction manual about military scouting and wilderness survival called *Aids to Scouting*.

His sudden fame fuelled the sales, and the book was particularly popular with young boys. He was inspired to write another version, specifically for his new demographic, and in 1908 the result was *Scouting for Boys*, which focused on survival techniques and left out the more military subjects. He focused on a different kind of hero instead – the heroes of the wilderness, such as backwoodsmen and explorers, followed later on by sailors and airmen.

Baden-Powell published *Scouting for Boys* in six fortnightly parts, setting out activities and programmes which existing youth organisations could use as a basis for their activities. The reaction was phenomenal.

In a very short time, Scout Patrols were created up and down the UK, all following the principles of Baden-Powell's book. In 1909, the first Scout Rally was held at Crystal Palace in London, which 11,000 Scouts attended.

Baden-Powell soon retired from the army and in 1910 he formed The Boy Scouts Association, and later The Girl Guides. By the time of The Boy Scouts Association's first census in 1910, it had over 100,000 Scouts.

The Boy Scout Movement established itself throughout the British Empire soon after the publication of *Scouting for Boys*. By 1908, Scouting was established in Gibraltar, Malta, Canada, Australia, New Zealand and South Africa. In 1909 Chile was the first country outside the British dominions to have a Scouting organisation, and in the same year the Scouting phenomenon spread to Belgium. The first Scout troop was founded in Brussels by Englishman Harold Parfitt. The Belgian version of this, the Boy Scouts of Belgium, was founded in 1910 in Brussels, using the British badges, rules and uniforms.

The scouts were a wildly popular, renegade phenomenon – empowering young boys, and later young girls, to learn new skills, to be independent and most of all, to go on adventures.

By the time Georges was 12, the scouts were more established, but still a relatively new and exciting group. A young Georges, bored of his grey neighbourhood that was overcoming the effects of the war, tired of his reserved parents and lack of freedom, couldn't wait to join.

In 1919, Georges enrolled in the Belgian Boy Scouts, and his life changed forever. The scouts opened up a world of adventure to him that he had only previously read about. The group Georges joined was a secular troop, as was his school at the time, which was unusual in the very Catholic area where he lived, and this exciting group left an indelible impression on the budding artist.

'My childhood seemed to me very grey,' Georges said in 1973. 'Of course, I have memories, but these do not begin to brighten, to become coloured, until the moment I discovered Scouting.'

Soon, however, Georges' father, Alexis, was encouraged by his boss, the old-fashioned traditionalist Henri Van Roye-Waucquez, to change Georges' school to a Catholic establishment, and even offered to pay the fees for them as he thought it would offer a better education.

Buckling under the pressure and keen to further their social standing, his parents moved him to Saint-Boniface secondary school, a Roman Catholic institution.

A year later, Georges was also forced to leave his Scouting group and instead join the Saint-Boniface secondary school's group, which was part of the Baden-Powell Association of Scouts of Belgium, but run by the Catholic Church.

Georges was upset to leave his group behind where he had made strong friendships, but also later spoke of the secular Scouting group as severely anti-religious and punctuated by brutal fights. He even alleged to one interviewer that there were group masturbation sessions in which the older boys led the younger ones to follow.

He slotted happily into the new Catholic Scouting group and it was here that he found adventure, companionship and fun. He was a natural leader, inspiring the other scouts and soon became troop leader of the Squirrel Patrol, earning the name 'Curious Fox' ('Renard Curieux').

With the Scouts, he travelled to summer camps in Italy, Switzerland, Austria and Spain, and in the summer of 1923 his troop hiked 200 miles across the Pyrenees. Georges loved the camping trips. He was, as his nickname suggested, a curious child and enjoyed exploring. He later said, 'We were getting away; camping and discovering the world. It was camaraderie, sport, adventure. I was a passionate Scout. The Pyrenees were the Tibet of my youth.'

His experiences with Scouting would have a significant influence on the rest of his life, sparking his love of the natural world, and providing him with a moral compass that prized personal loyalty and keeping one's promises above all else.

He would also meet friends that would stay with him for life, such as José De Launoit, who he would eventually work with at Studios Hergé, as well as Philippe Gérard, who would act as a scriptwriting consultant sometime later.

However, there were issues with the new Scouting group, too. There were allegations of abuse within the troop, where one of the scoutmasters would apparently trap angry horseflies under a glass on the skin of the young scouts to see how many bites they could stand. Georges, while having a deep love of Scouting, developed a hatred of authority and order, often repeating to himself, 'I am sure that God does not exist'.

As an escape from this, he would while the hours away sketching anything and everything that crossed his path. He would sketch on any piece of paper he came across, from his school books to scraps, which his friends, realising how talented Georges was, would preserve for years to come.

Aside from giving him the freedom to see his friends and have exciting adventures, Scouting most importantly gave him his first few crucial opportunities to publish his artwork. While he was sketching and doodling in a cartoon style one afternoon, one of his scoutmasters, René Weverbergh, noticed his incredible talent. Weverbergh encouraged the young artist, and printed one of his drawings in the newsletter of the Saint-Boniface Scouts, *Jamais Assez* (translated as 'Never Enough') which was Georges' first published work.

Weverbergh became involved in the publication of *Le Boy-Scout*, the official publication of the Belgian Catholic Scouts, and encouraged Georges to submit illustrations, which he would then duly publish. The first of these drawings appeared in the fifth issue of the magazine in 1922. Georges had just turned 15 and he wrote and illustrated an article on the lasso, something that would reappear in his work time and again.

Georges was involved in the Catholic Action movement, which was a group whose aim was to encourage a Catholic influence on society, but he would always say he 'never really had what people call faith'. Catholicism surrounded him, however, through school, scouts and the Catholic Action group, and embedded in him a strong sense of morality and the idea of sin, which he would struggle with as he became older.

It also gave him numerous opportunities to be published. He contributed many illustrations to *Le Blé qui Lève* (The wheat that grows), a Catholic publication for young Belgian people, as well as posters for events and adverts for *Le Campeur*, a Scout newspaper.

Drawing was taking up more and more of his time as he focused on publishing his work, but he managed to balance this with his studies at school. Indeed, he was very successful, winning accolades for excellence and he completed his secondary education at the top of his class. Despite his achievements, he was considered a corrupting force by his teachers, who were not so fond of the budding artist, due to his strong mischievous streak.

In 1924 Georges and his friend François Denis found a man hanging dead from a tree in the woods. A true entrepreneur, upon discovering this sight, the young Georges collected the rope and sold off pieces to his schoolmates for 25 centimes per centimetre. Clearly his Catholic morality did not interfere with business matters!

It was at this time that Georges started to try new ideas with his signature. He used a range of different options before settling on Hergé, which was created from reversing his initials to 'R.G'. For the young cartoonist this solved many issues; he could save his real name for the great art he had planned out for his future and he got rid of the 'Remi', which erased the family he was less than happy with and gave him true independence, a fresh slate with no history to hold him down. This new signature was used in the December issue of *Le Boy-Scout* for the first time and so 'Hergé' was born.

Chapter 2

Hergé finished school winning prizes for excellence, but without a plan for his future. University was not even considered and he was expected to get a job, preferably in the office with his father – but Hergé had no intention of taking on such a dull role.

He was still sketching constantly and had a girlfriend named Marie-Louise Van Cutsem, who was a childhood family friend. The pair were very much in love and often talked about getting engaged, but the girl's father was unimpressed with Hergé and his artistic ambitions. The young doodler was not good enough for his daughter and he soon put an end to the relationship, leaving the pair heartbroken.

Although his love life was faltering, it was around this time that Hergé got his first important career break. His work for Scouting publications led to a dream job for the 17-year-old – a role on *Le Boy Scout*, the national scouting magazine. For the young man whose main passions were Scouting and drawing, this was the perfect role and he eagerly set to work. One of his early illustrations for the magazine was a Scout Patrol Leader named Totor, an early prototype of Tintin.

Scouting was an incredibly important part of his life at this stage, and instilled in Hergé the Scouting instincts and morals that would filter through all of his future work.

Hergé's mentor and old scoutmaster, René Weverbergh, was a journalist on the staff of *Le Boy Scout*, and was very impressed with the 17-year-old's work. He subsequently recommended him to *Le Vingtième Siècle*, a major Catholic newspaper, where Hergé worked initially in the subscriptions department, starting on 1 September 1925.

The offices of *Le Vingtième Siècle* were set in a large building in the centre of a fashionable area of Brussels. The newspaper was well known as a hub for financial and political news, told through a very distinct Catholic slant. Strong Catholic morals were at the centre of the agenda. It was nationalistic, hostile to Communists, democracy and non-Catholics alike, and never printed anything that went against Catholic customs.

Hergé had lived in a very Catholic area all his life, and having been raised as a Catholic by his parents and attended a Catholic school, this paper was a comfortable place for him, despite his lack of faith. However, the work bored him to tears and he spent his free time indulging his passion and continued to draw for *Le Boy-Scout* and other small newspapers.

At one point, the job became too much for him. He was so disenchanted with the monotonous duties at *Le Vingtième Siècle* that one day he simply failed to turn up. This would become a familiar hallmark of his working pattern – once he didn't enjoy something, he would always find it extremely difficult to carry on. He was summoned back to work at the newspaper, and he duly complied, but he soon found a new way to escape, by enlisting for military service in August 1926.

Hergé thought this was the answer he was looking for – the comradery and activities of the scouts, time to draw, and a way out of the dull subscriptions department he had been languishing in.

But military service was not the enjoyable escape he had hoped for. He was bored and wrote letters home to his family to complain about the vile hygiene of the barracks, the filthiness and the stench. He missed his family, particularly his mother. He described himself as a soldier boy, and struggled being so far from home.

Luckily for Hergé, he was allowed to leave the barracks and return home fairly soon, where he continued his military service until he was discharged in 1927. As he reached the end of his stint of military service, the thought of going back to work at the subscriptions department for *Le Vingtième Siècle* was too much for the easily bored Hergé, so he arranged a meeting with the editor, Abbot Norbert Wallez, to discuss his future.

Norbert Wallez was a Belgian priest and journalist, who would have an enormous influence on the young protégé. He was larger than life in stature and personality. The son of a farmer, Wallez was ordained a priest in 1906 and he devoted himself to teaching. While working as a teacher, he started to contribute to *La Metropole*, a Catholic newspaper of Antwerp, and he found his true passion: journalism.

During the First World War, he enlisted as a volunteer, and returned to teach at the religious Bonne Espérance school and at the School of Commerce in Mons. It was here, in 1924, that Cardinal Désiré-Joseph Mercier asked him to take over editorship of the struggling *Le Vingtième*

Siècle. Wallez leapt at the chance. The paper had a dwindling circulation, but he soon whipped it into shape and the figures shot up.

Le Vingtième Siècle was run by the Catholic Party and linked with the *Catholic Review of Ideas and Events*. For both conservative publications, political unity in Belgium was extremely important.

Meanwhile, Benito Mussolini's actions in Italy caught Wallez's attention. It was in 1923 that Mussolini started placing crucifixes in schools and other public buildings, and Wallez was impressed. He travelled to Italy and managed to arrange an appointment with Mussolini. This was one of the defining moments of his life and he returned more of a fan of the regime than ever. He proudly placed an autographed portrait of the Fascist dictator on his desk, dedicated 'to Norbert Wallez, a friend of Italy and of Fascism, with friendship, 1924'.

For Wallez, Italy displayed the ideal form of Catholicism, and he managed to ignore the darker side of the regime. Wallez came home determined to espouse his ideas for Belgium with vigour, which he wrote in his book, *Belgium and the Rhineland*. Here he denounced politicians, and blamed foreigners, especially Jews, for any issues within the country, reserving a particular hatred for Israel. He wanted to see the federation of Belgium and the Rhineland, a region of Germany that he considered essentially Catholic.

Wallez was a charismatic man with strong, racist views that would not be tolerated today. In 1920s Belgium, the country was in a mess after the Berlin stock market crash of 1912. Jewish people were being blamed for the financial disaster, and so Wallez's views resonated with some, although he was very much a polarising character and was equally hated by others.

However unpalatable his views were, the larger-than-life abbot, who was more interested in politics and journalism than religion, formed an indelible impression on Hergé – setting the wheels in motion for him to become one of the most famous cartoonists of all time.

When Hergé came back from military service, it was Wallez he approached with his unhappiness at the thought of returning to the rather dull subscriptions department. He requested a change and the young cartoonist clearly fought his case well, as the day after he was discharged from military service, he received a letter from Wallez offering him a three-year contract as a fully-fledged photographic reporter and cartoonist. He was given a press pass, railway pass and an allowance for expenses, as well as a salary of 600 francs per month.

Hergé spent his time working in the darkroom and created illustrations for the editorial and advertising departments in his small mezzanine office, churning out whatever was required at speed. 'I did anything and everything,' he would say of this exciting time in his life. It was the perfect training ground for the budding cartoonist.

While Hergé was cautious and unsure of himself, Wallez soon became a father figure to his young charge, pushing him to read more and to be the best he could be.

Hergé continued to draw *The Adventures of Totor* for *Le Boy-Scout* alongside his work for the newspaper, which involved illustrating a range of stories. His favourite work was illustrating the literary pages, where the likes of Leo Tolstoy and Felix Salten's *Bambi* were featured.

When the offices of *Le Vingtième Siècle* were reorganised, Hergé left his tiny office and moved to a large, airy space above Abbot Wallez. Working near Wallez was his secretary, Germaine Kieckens, who had joined the paper in February 1928 after Hergé had returned from his military service.

Hergé had a crush on this red-headed woman, who was a year older than him, but she was not interested. She thought he was far too immature for her, and would call him 'my young friend'.

Hergé did not give up and continued to pursue Germaine. During all the long hours working at close quarters, he obviously worked his charm as she eventually agreed to go on a date with him, and they went rowing with two other friends from the newspaper. After a couple more dates, Hergé visited Germaine at the beach where she was spending her summer holiday with her family.

It was definitely not love at first sight for the pair. Germaine explained to Hergé that she had suffered a bad break-up just before she had met him and was not ready for a new relationship. The two were quite distant with each other to begin with and took things slowly.

Meanwhile, Hergé threw himself into his job, sometimes working seven days a week, skipping lunch and staying late at the office. He would never leave without saying goodbye to the abbot, who he was growing closer and closer to. Wallez took Hergé under his wing and would teach him about different aspects of culture, literature and politics. Hergé had never had a figure like this in his life before and he hung on his mentor's every word.

Always a visionary, Wallez decided to produce a new separate section of the newspaper just for children, and he gave his protégé Hergé the opportunity of a lifetime – to create and edit this supplement, which would be called *Le Petit Vingtième*.

Hergé couldn't believe his luck – this was a world away from the subscriptions department! The pair set out their plans for the new section in an announcement in the main newspaper, and said it would be 'interesting, lively, educational and beautifully illustrated'. However, with a short time frame and a lack of resources, the first few issues would fall far short of the lofty aspirations.

For the first ten weeks of the supplement, Hergé illustrated and published two comic strips per issue of *The Extraordinary Adventures of Flup, Nenesse, Pousette and Cochonnet*, which by most standards were anything but extraordinary. It was the tale of three children and their inflatable pig, written by Desmedt, the sports columnist on the main newspaper.

Hergé was not happy. The story was dull and he could not bring himself to spend a great deal of time on something so inadequate, so the illustrations were quick and slapdash. Even at this stage, Hergé wanted control over the whole process, and was not happy with anything other than perfection.

After the unfulfilling experience of illustrating someone else's story, Hergé decided to take control and only used the ideas of others when absolutely necessary – he was much happier doing everything himself.

He was still working full-time for *Le Vingtième Siècle*, as well as illustrating the literary supplement and he was now responsible for this new and exciting project, but he was always on the lookout for something new.

When he discovered a pile of Mexican newspapers sent over by one of *Le Vingtième Siècle*'s correspondents, history was made. In these newspapers were syndicated American comic strips such as *Bringing Up Father* by George McManus and *Krazy Kat* by George Herriman. It was here he discovered the use of the speech bubble, something that would revolutionise the comic strip in Belgium. At the time, this mechanism was rarely used in Europe, but fairly common in the States.

In 1928, Hergé published his first comic strip in an issue of *The Whistle* using the new method of the speech bubble. He also incorporated some of the other techniques from the American comics, such as characters with small noses, as well as a similar kind of humour – and his iconic style was set.

Abbot Wallez saw a copy of the newspaper and loved it, but more importantly, he wanted it for *Le Petit Vingtième*. He immediately asked Hergé to write and illustrate his own story using the characters from one of the scenes in the previous comic strip – a young boy and his white dog.

It was hastily assembled; he chose the name for his hero without much thought, and used the nickname of his old girlfriend, 'Milou', for the dog, as an affectionate aside, which was known in English-speaking countries as 'Snowy'.

The young boy from the comic strip had appeared before in the Totor work Hergé had made some years earlier. He scrambled a comic strip together, redesigned the character and renamed him – and so Tintin was created.

The muse for Tintin was undoubtedly his younger brother, Paul, who was 16 at the time, and bore more than a passing resemblance to the character. Hergé later said, 'My childhood playmate was my brother who was five years younger than I. I watched him a lot, he entertained and fascinated me. It makes sense that Tintin took on his character, gesture, poses.'

Hergé decided that the new character would be a reporter, having spent long hours in *Le Vingtième Siècle*'s offices watching the reporters of the time whisking in and out after travelling to far-flung places.

Wallez dictated that the first adventure would be set in Soviet Russia, and Hergé dutifully complied. On 10 January 1929, the inaugural comic strip for one of the greatest comic series of all time appeared in *Le Petit Vingtième*. It was the opening for *Tintin in the Land of the Soviets* and history was made.

The reaction to this new comic strip, the new format and the characters was unprecedented. It was loved by the French and the Belgians, and soon the circulation started to soar on the day the new instalment of the Tintin adventure was published.

The comic strip treated the Soviet Union with scorn, with Hergé taking much of his inspiration for the themes of the story from a book Wallez had given him. He had handed over *Starless Moscow* by Joseph Douillet, a very popular book at the time, and asked Hergé to pass on the details to the young readers through the comic strip.

Starless Moscow was deeply disparaging of all things Russian. While Hergé was clearly influenced by this, he was already quite biased towards the country. He had been shocked and disgusted at the massacre of the Russian Imperial Romanov family under the instructions of the Bolsheviks in 1918, and it was this incident that prompted him to produce anti-Communist sketches earlier in *The Whistle* paper.

His mentor Wallez was a staunch critic of the Soviets, and he was not the only one. A great number of Belgians at the time were labouring under a generally anti-Communist cloud of disapproval, and the Tintin story captured their feeling perfectly.

Although Hergé's style developed exponentially over time, the beginnings of the great series were already present in those first few comic strips. We see the main character, a young fellow with basic features and no surname, history or family, in a purely slapstick adventure, with a dash of damning political critique that would be the hallmark (and downfall) of some of his later work.

Hergé never thought this character would be the start of greatness for him; he actually believed this first adventure of Tintin's would be the last. The story begins with the young Belgian reporter, Tintin, and his dog Snowy being sent to report on the current affairs of the Soviet Union. Throughout the adventure, the Soviet secret police try to kill him, to silence the foreign journalist, but Tintin miraculously thwarts their plans.

The propaganda is strong and unsubtle in the story. Tintin exposes all the 'secrets' of Stalin's Bolshevik government – the Soviet factories they pretend are running, when in reality there are workers behind the scenes burning bundles of straw and clanging metal to make it seem as though they are operational. Tintin also witnesses a local election in which the Bolsheviks threaten the voters to make sure they win. He then goes to Moscow, which he describes as 'a stinking slum', where they find a government official handing out bread to homeless Marxists, while refusing to help non-Marxists.

It is a damning portrayal of the Soviet Union, and the political bias is especially strong for a children's comic strip, but there is plenty of slapstick humour to dilute the underlying message Wallez wanted to disseminate.

There's a great deal of movement in the fast-paced story and very little text, so it had a rather cinematic quality and children adored the series from the very start. Talking movies began in 1927 with the production of *The Jazz Singer* and Hergé had watched the new development with great interest. He always referred to his comics as films, and he would later say, 'One hundred per cent sound and talking films, of course.'

It is also in this inaugural story that Tintin gets his trademark quiff. He starts the adventure with flat hair, but after a particularly fast car chase, he gets his iconic hairstyle, and it would stay like that forever more.

Buoyed by the positive response from readers, Hergé and Wallez increased the publicity for the series. In *Le Petit Vingtième* on April Fools' Day 1930, Wallez printed a letter from the GPU, the Russian State Secret Police, written by Hergé and decorated with hammers and sickles. The letter warned the newspaper to stop publishing Tintin's reports 'which are nothing but a series of attacks against the Soviets' and ended with, 'The choice is yours: the end of this news campaign, or death.'

The editor, Hergé again, replied with bravado: 'We are not frightened of these threats, our duty as an independent Catholic newspaper being always to condemn a regime of terror like Russian Bolshevism. Our young readers should rest assured that the story of Tintin will continue to appear as always until Tintin comes back from that foreign land, having, we hope, escaped from every trap set in his path.'

Wallez was overjoyed with the boy reporter and staged a flamboyant publicity event for Tintin's return to Brussels from Moscow. On 24 April, an article announced Tintin's return and encouraged the readers to go and meet him as he arrived at the train station in the capital.

The pair searched for a young actor to play Tintin and found a suitable boy in a Scouting troop near Brussels – the 15-year-old Lucien Peppermans. After being sent for two haircuts, he was deemed acceptable, although Hergé, ever critical, thought his head was too big.

Having hurriedly changed into his costume in the bathroom of the train station, and applied liberal amounts of hair products to try to keep the trademark quiff in place, Lucien stepped off the train as Tintin in the Gare du Nord with a suitcase bearing a large 'Moscow' sticker and Snowy at his side to a sea of cheering fans, largely made up of Catholic Boy Scouts, whose support Hergé could always rely on.

He was escorted through the masses to the offices of *Le Vingtième Siècle* in a Buick convertible where he delivered a speech, written for him by Hergé, to a very enthusiastic crowd of fans. The main paper, *Le Vingtième Siècle*, covered the spectacle and Tintin became a star.

Wallez didn't stop there. He had big plans for the boy reporter, and the next idea was to sell the story in book form, which was a huge success and sold 10,000 copies. The Abbot, who was commercially ahead of his time, also ran a limited edition of 500 copies, which were numbered and signed by Tintin and Snowy. Hergé provided Tintin's signature, with Germaine Kieckens at his side, adding a little dog-signature on behalf of Snowy. Germaine later said, 'It was the Abbot who suggested all of it. He really was an exceptional human being.'

At this time Hergé and Germaine were becoming closer and closer, but Hergé was aware that Germaine looked up enormously to the Abbot, who would never be able to reciprocate her feelings. They continued to work harmoniously together and the relationship between the cartoonist and Germaine began to blossom slowly but surely.

While the first Tintin story was a great success, the crude subject matter would haunt Hergé, who later admitted to finding his first full-length comic strip extremely embarrassing, and referred to it as 'a transgression of his youth'. He refused to allow republication until 1973. The Abbot, on the other hand, was not embarrassed, and had many more ideas for Tintin, and also for Hergé.

In the meantime, although Tintin was a huge hit for the paper, Hergé was not treated like a star at all and he was expected to continue with all his usual duties. He now had help on *Le Petit Vingtième*, however, first in the form of Eugene Van Nyverseel until he left for military service. Then in March 1930, Paul Jamin, also known as 'Jam', joined Hergé as a collaborator. He had been classmates with Hergé's brother, Paul, and Hergé and Jamin would become lifelong friends.

Jam started by doing basic work such as erasing marks, tracing frames and working on tinting, before moving on to creating illustrations and covers of his own, as well as writing a column under the name of 'Uncle Jo', who was supposed to be an old man with a long white beard.

Hergé and Jam were kindred spirits and enjoyed the boisterous atmosphere of *Le Vingtième Siècle*, with the odd characters Abbot Wallez had collected together, and loved nothing more than playing pranks on each other. They travelled to Paris for a festival and although they were supposed to stay in the hotel with a church connection that had been arranged for them, they spent a night in the rather less than religious Moulin Rouge.

While Abbot Wallez turned a blind eye to their antics, it was at this time that he encouraged Hergé to produce another comic strip, which resulted in *Quick and Flupke*, two kids from Brussels causing chaos wherever they went, possibly based on the comradery of Hergé and Jam. This shorter weekly comic strip was popular, but never reached the same levels of popularity as Tintin.

Hergé had strong ideas about the direction Tintin should take from here, and it was west-bound to the USA to show the issues the Red Indians faced. Wallez was extraordinarily puzzled by Hergé's suggestion – this was far too left-wing for the ultraconservative fascist! He knew where Tintin was headed next, and the story would not involve teepees or lassos…

Chapter 3

What resulted from their heated discussions was instead *Tintin in the Congo*, possibly the most objectionable of the Tintin canon in terms of violence, stereotyping and general racism.

The Belgian Congo was a relatively new State, only created in 1908. Previously, in 1885, King Leopold II had taken control of the Congo despite reservations from the Belgian government, and created a personal colony with his own army, using a great deal of violence, which he then named the Congo Free State.

The Congo Free State operated as a corporate state, which was privately controlled by the ambitious Leopold II through the Association Internationale Africaine. Under his control, the Congolese were ruthlessly and violently exploited, and millions were killed.

The King ran a private army called the Force Publique which made the local people work as forced labour, while reaping all the resources from the country. The army would kill and abuse people randomly and viciously.

The appalling conditions in the Congo Free State under Leopold's control were exposed in the early 1900s by the Casement Report, and widely publicised in the British, European and American press. The situation was a major embarrassment, and Leopold came under intense pressure to end his personal rule. The Belgian government stepped in to make the country an official colony of Belgium in 1908, and it was renamed the Belgian Congo.

In 1930s Belgium, there were conflicting reports of what was actually happening in what was now the Belgian Congo.

For Wallez, the area was ripe with possibility, and he was keen to extol the virtues of the country. He wanted to highlight the positives of colonialism to the young readers of *Le Petit Vingtième*, which is why he insisted on sending Tintin to the Congo for his next adventure. Wallez was adamant that Hergé should inspire his young readers to find out more about the Congo and encourage them to go and work there in the future.

Hergé, however, was not enthused with the subject matter. He wasn't interested in the area and he knew little of what life was like in the Belgian Congo. His remit, he felt, was purely to draw fast and funny stories to engage Belgian children and turn them into lifelong *Le Vingtième* readers.

With his very basic research consisting of a visit to a local museum – the Museum of the Congo in Tervuren – and seeking tales from newspaper reporters who had visited the area, he set to work. The resulting story was simplistic and featured extremely racist and violent scenes.

Tintin and Snowy are sent to the Belgian Congo on a reporting expedition. The pair encounter various Congolese people and wild animals, and get into a variety of slapstick-driven scrapes. Tintin eventually uncovers a diamond smuggling operation masterminded by the American gangster, Al Capone.

The story was once again a big success in Belgium, and Wallez was extremely happy with the work of his young protégé. In later years, *Tintin in the Congo* became a controversial subject due to the racist colonial overtones, as well as the violence towards animals and the glorification of hunting. A particularly gratuitous scene involves Tintin drilling a hole in a rhinoceros, and filling it with dynamite, before blowing the poor creature up.

Hergé would later say, 'I didn't like the colonists, who came back bragging about their exploits, but I couldn't prevent myself from seeing the Blacks as big children, either.' He also said in an interview, 'I'm very permeable, very impressionable, which makes me an excellent medium. All my books carry the traces of the time when they were drawn. For Tintin in the Congo, the fact is that I was fed on the prejudices of the bourgeois society I lived in. It was 1930. The only things I knew about these countries were what people said about them at the time. Africans were no more than big children. "It's lucky for them that we're over there," and so on. I drew Africans along these lines in the purely paternalistic spirit of the times in Belgium.'

Despite its unsophisticated narrative and simplistic humour, *Tintin in the Congo* was very popular with children. The comic strip ended on 11 June 1931 and Wallez, who was thrilled with the results of his brainchild, was busy arranging another extravagant stunt to celebrate. In the weeks before the comic strip finished, *Le Petit Vingtième* promoted the return of Tintin and Snowy with 'Uncle Jo' regularly discussing the upcoming event.

When the day came, fans swamped the Gare du Nord again to greet their hero. This time, a different actor was used for 'Tintin', as the previous boy, Lucien Peppermans, had grown too tall. So, it was a much younger Henri Dendoncker dressed as Tintin who arrived in Brussels alongside ten Congolese people, as well as a whole host of animals borrowed from a circus.

A crowd of more than 5,000 also congregated around the headquarters of the newspaper where staff were distributing sweets and African souvenirs. They arranged the same event in Liège in eastern Belgium, where a riot nearly ensued.

The whole event was slicker and more commercially-minded this time around, with the book already printed and ready to be sold on the big day. It was a huge success and Wallez couldn't be happier. He increased Hergé's salary which had started at 600 francs a month to 2,000.

Hergé was pleased with the success of the story and the recognition from his boss and mentor, but in later years, he admitted to being embarrassed by this particular tale. He was reluctant to keep the book in print due to the many offensive scenes, only eventually allowing it to be republished due to the continuing popularity.

However, due to the success of *Tintin in the Congo*, Hergé was given free rein over the next story. Wallez had finally given in to the cartoonist and allowed him to take the boy reporter wherever he wanted, so Tintin was at last heading to America.

Work-wise, everything was going well for Hergé, but his private life left a lot to be desired. The 24-year-old was still living at home with his family in a tiny attic room with a small round window, and his love life was going nowhere.

He was still smitten with Germaine, who he saw all the time in the offices and often collaborated with her. While Hergé would walk her home every night, and much as she enjoyed his company, she did not consider him marriage material as she was looking for an older, more mature man – someone more in the mould of her boss, Abbot Wallez.

Hergé was living at home and very much the young dandy wearing sharp tailored suits made by his mother. He was a prankster at heart and still extremely fond of the scouts, definitely not the cultured and refined man Germaine pined for. But his career was beginning to take off – he started to exhibit his work in galleries in Belgium and was interviewed in a couple of magazines. He was beginning to grow into the type of sophisticated man she could be interested in.

At this time Abbot Wallez had taken to encouraging the young pair to marry. As a mentor to both Hergé and Germaine, he was an extremely influential figure and this pressure was taken seriously by both of them.

And it wasn't just Germaine and Hergé he was hounding to find a partner; Abbot Wallez was persuading everyone to tie the knot at this time. At one point he called a meeting and spoke to all single employees of the newspaper, ordering them to find husbands or wives.

Whether the meddling abbot was a factor or not, it was in 1931 that Hergé's relationship with Germaine started to blossom. They would exchange long letters, full of feeling and emotion, but he was becoming despondent and unsure of how he should proceed. At Easter time he sought guidance from Father Edouard Neut at the Saint-Andre abbey in Bruges, where he had spent time on a retreat after finishing high school.

Hergé found the meeting an enormous help and wrote a long letter to Germaine to explain what he had learned. He told her how the priest was able to see into his heart so clearly, how he had the vision to see what Hergé was truly missing and longing for – and it was her. He confessed his deep attraction to her, and explained that he realised he needed to make changes to himself to be the person she wanted.

After his openness, the pair became much closer and a more romantic bond developed between them. Germaine went to Bruges to visit him while he stayed at the abbey and they went on day trips together. In May, they travelled to Paris with Hergé's parents and visited all the major attractions, from the Eiffel Tower to the Arc de Triomphe.

Later in the year, they spent a day at the beach together and he would doodle and write in a sketch book how much she meant to him. He told her how happy she made him and she filled his life, which had been empty without her. He was very much in love with Germaine, later writing long passionate letters telling her how much he had changed, and that she was the catalyst, the instigating factor in this. He felt she had changed him for the better.

Germaine responded to his passionate words with more passion and would write long letters back to him, clearly swept up in the emotional exchange. However, much later in life, Germaine confessed that she had not been that interested in marrying Hergé.

Her suitor, though, was very keen and the Abbot continued to pressure the singletons in the office. Soon the couple were engaged. Germaine's parents held a lavish engagement party at their home in Laeken on 21 February 1932 to celebrate the announcement, and the pair were very happy, along with the pushy Abbot.

While Hergé was finally content in his love life, he began to set his sights on another goal – he wanted a career he could be proud of. *Tintin in the Congo* had been a great success, but Hergé was not happy with his work. He was determined that *Tintin in America* would be different. It was a project Hergé was passionate about, an exercise in nostalgia for the keen scout, with the Red Indians recalling elements of his Scouting days, as well as the films he had loved to watch as a child.

He researched more thoroughly than he had for either of his previous works. Through a mixture of magazines such as the satirical *Le Crapouillot*, which showcased images of American skyscrapers, and books including *Scènes de la Vie Future*, which depicted the slaughterhouses of Chicago, he started to become interested in perfecting the details of the backgrounds in his work and making them as accurate as possible.

Originally called *Tintin in Chicago*, the story was meant to include Tintin defeating the Chicago crime syndicates, but soon, however, the boss escapes to the Wild West and Tintin follows suit. So Hergé got to write his Wild West story after all, heavily influenced by his Scouting days, which had revolved around camps and tents, warpaint and arrows, as well as all the other accoutrements that had accompanied the carefree hours in the Scouting troop.

Tintin pursues the gangster across the country, where he encounters a tribe of Blackfoot Native Americans before he eventually captures the criminals and defeats the crime syndicate.

The book has several digs at Americans, especially about the shoddy treatment of the Red Indians. In one scene, an oil spring is found on the land belonging to the Native American tribe. Prospectors appear immediately and, thinking the land belongs to Tintin, they offer tens of thousands of dollars. When they realise it is the Red Indians' property, they offer 25 dollars and shuffle the tribe along. In a matter of hours, the area has been developed beyond recognition.

Hergé also comments on police corruption with scenes depicting Tintin being treated brutally by the officers for attempting to report the criminals. And there are digs at American capitalism, too; when Tintin delivers the crime boss Bobby Smiles to the police, he is hailed as a hero and offered sponsorship from a myriad of different groups.

Keen to highlight the plight of the Native Americans, Hergé made this a priority in the storyline, and Wallez's anti-capitalism stance slotted in very well alongside. Once again, the story was a roaring success, and when Wallez orchestrated the third 'homecoming' event for Tintin, they drew the biggest crowds yet.

Due to the popularity of the series, various publishers began to show an interest in the character – and also in Hergé. In April 1932, one of Hergé's former colleagues, Charles Lesne, who had just moved to work for Louis Casterman at his publishing house, Casterman, was keen to introduce Hergé to his new boss.

Hergé met with Casterman to discuss publishing opportunities with them and very quickly the publisher became the official printer of the Tintin books developed from the comic strips in *Le Petit Vingtième*. This was a relationship and collaboration that would last throughout Hergé's life.

While Hergé was busy arranging new contracts and deals and developing his career, in his free time, he and Germaine were also planning their wedding which was fast approaching.

Hergé and Germaine married at the Saint-Roch church in Laeken on 20 July 1932 surrounded by a host of friends and family, and with their boss and mentor, Abbot Wallez, officiating at the ceremony. Hergé was 25 years old, Germaine was 26.

However much the Abbot had encouraged the two to marry and however much affection he had for the pair, he was still a hard taskmaster and had made them work late the night before the wedding to finish duties at the newspaper. After the big day, the pair went on a much-needed honeymoon in Vianden, a beautiful town in Luxembourg.

When they returned to Brussels, the happy couple went house-hunting and finally chose a cosy apartment on the second floor of a building that was still being built in Schaerbeek, along rue Knapen, on the outskirts of town.

Hergé found space in the little apartment for a makeshift office and worked more and more from home. He was constantly sketching images from their life together in pencil or watercolour, usually of his new wife, who he adored. He would draw Germaine reclining in bed, cooking their dinner, or playing with their Siamese cat called Thaïke. He also drew a series of nude images in red chalk, which was a new direction for Hergé in terms of his art. He was clearly smitten with his new wife.

Indeed, they had a lot in common – they had both had a relatively unhappy childhood. Germaine's parents were rather elderly and having lost a child before she came along, were very overprotective of her, which she had found quite stifling. They were both ambitious; Germaine wanted to be an actress, but this was an ambition that would remain unfulfilled, while Hergé's career soared. And as they both counted Abbot Wallez as their mentor, he shaped their ideas about the world and had also been a major catalyst for their marriage.

They loved spending time together and Hergé would take reams of photos of the budding actress in various poses. The next year, they went on holiday with another couple to the Pyrenees. For Hergé this was familiar territory from his Scouting days, although the dynamic was different with partners coming along too. They went hiking and camped in tents, shuffling together meals as best as they could. Hergé was in his element, but for Germaine this was a complete nightmare, and she never went on a similar trip again. Hergé would rely on his Scouting groups for this kind of adventure in the future.

Life was good for Hergé. He was happily married to a woman he loved, he had a lovely apartment and his work was exciting – he couldn't ask for more. But it was not to last.

In 1933, he was dealt his first professional blow. *Le Vingtième Siècle* printed a series of damning articles on construction problems with the Albert Canal. The language was particularly strong, and while the newspaper was never a publication to shy away from controversy, on this occasion it was deemed it had gone too far.

The director-general of the Bureau of Public Works, Mr Delmer, was furious. He stormed into *Le Vingtième*'s offices complaining he had been defamed and tried to start a fight with Wallez. Wallez did not fight back and Delmer was physically removed from the building by a group of journalists.

Delmer was so incensed at the way he had been treated that he took *Le Vingtième Siècle* to court. He lost the case, but the damage had been done. Regardless of the outcome, the owners of the newspaper were upset that their moralistic publication had been embroiled in this kind of scandal; they forced Abbot Wallez to resign from the position he cherished so much and he was sent to work in a tiny parish in Charleroi.

Hergé was devastated. He had lost his mentor and friend, the first person to introduce him to a more intellectual life, the person who had believed in him and ignited his career, the person who had facilitated his marriage to Germaine. He felt less and less attached to the newspaper now that the abbot had gone, and began to think about a different direction for his future.

At this time, he had a great deal of work creating advertisements and was well regarded in this field. In 1931 he had formed a collaborative group with a couple of friends that they had called 'Hergé Studios', which provided adverts for a range of smaller companies such as local shops, with more clients being added all the time.

By 1934 'Hergé Studios' was incorporated and initially comprised Hergé, Jose De Launoir and Adrien Jacquemotte, but the group often descended into arguments. Just months later, the company was dissolved following the latest disagreement, and then reformed without Jacquemotte.

The company did well, with Hergé's skills in advertising very much in evidence during the 1930s. He loved the creativity of the work, but in that period the Tintin stories would always take precedence.

Chapter 4

Tintin was about to set off for his new adventure. It was announced in *Le Petit Vingtième* on 24 November 1932 that Tintin had his sights set on new and exciting horizons.

In this new story, Tintin and Snowy take a well-deserved holiday, travelling to Port Said in Egypt, when they are pulled into a mystery. After meeting the eccentric Sophocles Sarcophagus, they discover a pharaoh's tomb full of mummified Egyptologists, as well as boxes of cigars labelled with a strange symbol. To unravel the mystery, they travel to Arabia and India, eventually uncovering a gang of international drug smugglers.

The story was inspired by the discovery of Tutankhamun's tomb in 1922, and the stories in the newspapers concerning the 'Curse of the Pharaohs', where a curse is supposedly cast upon anyone who disturbs the mummy of an Ancient Egyptian person, and causes bad luck, sickness or even death.

In terms of style, this book is a world away from *Tintin in America* and everything that had gone before. Rather than a series of loosely connected comic strips, which were very clearly an assembly of weekly adventures, this had a coherent narrative with one main plot, and signifies the true beginning of the style that marked Hergé out as an iconic cartoonist.

Some of the scenes show his remarkable talent emerging, such as the inspired dream-like sequence in the tomb and the eerie scene in the Indian house. In this adventure, both Hergé and Tintin had matured and this resulted in a story with more drama and greater narrative cohesion.

The mystery of the plot also marks a departure for Hergé from the previous three adventures. He was capturing the zeitgeist, as the 1930s were a time when mystery novels were becoming popular, with the works of Agatha Christie and Raymond Chandler erupting on to the scene.

Even though he knew he wanted to create a mystery story and he knew that these were usually intricately plotted, Hergé still set out on this new adventure without a plan. He said in an interview with Numa Sadoul, 'I wanted to try my hand at mystery, the detective novel, suspense, and I got myself so entangled in my enigmas that I almost couldn't get out again.'

The story was originally known as *Tintin in the Orient* in *Le Petit Vingtième*, but became *Cigars of the Pharaoh* in book form, and from the very beginning the readers were involved in the story and the direction it would take. An announcement was made in the paper calling for readers to write in with their ideas for who the mysterious enemies of Tintin were and also asking who could solve the story.

This was an enormous success with thousands of children writing in with their suggestions. Hergé certainly had a flair for publicity and knew exactly how to engage with his young readers; this was a helpful technique to gauge what they wanted and was also useful in progressing the plot when he found himself in a dead end.

Cigars of the Pharaoh is also a turning point for Hergé as important new characters are introduced and developed, such as Oliveira da Figueira, a Portuguese merchant. It was due to the friendly salesman from Lisbon that the Tintin books started to be translated – into Portuguese, of course.

The twins, Thomson and Thompson, were also introduced in this story. The two bungling detectives were determined to capture Tintin at all costs after a substantial reward was offered. Loosely based on Hergé's father, Alexis Remi, and his Uncle Léon, the pair would prove to be a big hit, and would reappear in the Tintin books time and time again.

The main character in this story was Sophocles Sarcophagus, an Egyptologist. Although he didn't make it into any other Tintin stories, he did act as an early prototype for the popular character that appears in later books, Professor Cuthbert Calculus, introduced in *Red Rackham's Treasure*.

The evil enemy in *Cigars of the Pharaoh* was someone who would become more and more important as time went on, and someone who would cause Hergé no end of issues – Roberto Rastapopoulos.

Hergé later said, 'Rastapopoulos isn't meant to represent anyone in particular. It all started with the name, which was suggested to me by a friend, and the character grew up around the name. Rastapopoulos, for me, is more or less a shady Mediterranean Greek… a stateless person, that is, according to my perspective at the time. One more detail: he is not Jewish.' However, he was certainly perceived to be Jewish and later on this would cause a furore around Hergé, as well as the entire Tintin series.

At the time of *Cigars of the Pharaoh*, there was a trickle of news filtering through to Belgium about the movements of the Nazis in Germany. By the end of 1932, the Nazi Party had the highest number of seats in the German Reichstag and were making strong inroads into the political sphere. Hitler was appointed Chancellor in January 1933, and they developed the one-party dictatorship of Nazi Germany soon after. Hitler's anti-Semitic rhetoric and plan to eliminate Jews from Germany was now reported across the world – he was angry at the post-First World War international order set by Britain and France, and wanted to establish a New Order.

In the offices of *Le Petit Vingtième*, they didn't quite know what to make of all this, and the reporting of what was happening was confused at best. On the one hand they criticised Hitler's actions with reports such as, 'Jews, Marxists, communists, and in general anyone who does not cry "Heil Hitler!" while standing stiffly at attention are being sent by the thousands to "concentration camps". Even Germans are being sent now, Aryan and non-Aryan, who dare to listen to radio transmissions from Moscow.'

But there was also a pervasive anti-Semitism within the pages. When they announced that Hitler would be limiting the persecution of the Jews, they also added, 'Let us hope that he will allow the many Jews exiled to our country to return to Germany, so that we will hear something other than Yiddish spoken on the beautiful streets of Brussels.'

While the political landscape was changing around them, work continued. In December 1933, Charles Lesne at Casterman Publishers approached Hergé with a proposal, asking if Casterman could launch the Tintin series in France – a potentially huge new market. Hergé was very keen on the idea, but he was still under contract with Abbot Wallez for three more books, despite the fact that his mentor had left the newspaper, so he couldn't make any changes at that stage.

Hergé was becoming disillusioned with the newspaper, trapped by the contract and unable to pursue the work he believed in. As he finished the latest comic strip in *Le Petit Vingtième* on 8 February 1934, it was due to be published in book form through Casterman.

In March of 1934, Charles Lesne sent him another contract to try to lure him away again. The contract concerned the publishing of *Cigars of the Pharaoh* and offered the cartoonist 3 francs per copy sold up to 10,000 with 2 francs per copy after that. It also gave the publishing house exclusive right of sale in Belgium and abroad, and said they would publish *Quick and Flupke* in book form in Belgium.

It was generally a good deal, with Hergé reaping an unusually large 15 per cent. It was no doubt that this tempting offer put his work at *Le Petit Vingtième* into perspective and he realised he had other viable options.

Spurred on by this, he sent a letter to his boss at *Le Petit Vingtième* saying that he was resigning. He told him he didn't think he'd be able to develop his career in the way he wished while working for them and felt stunted by the contract he had. Time was ticking by and he was keen to move forward and make his mark.

At this point, Hergé was still in charge of *Le Petit Vingtième*, which was by now a separate entity to the main paper. The new director, Mr Herinckx, did not want to lose him and negotiated with the cartoonist until they eventually struck a deal on 1 November.

Hergé came out of the negotiations very successfully with his salary rising from two thousand to three thousand francs a month. He now also had the freedom to work from home and his duties were reduced from being responsible for the entire publication to simply the cover illustrations and the Tintin and *Quick and Flupke* comic strips each week. Jam took over the rest of the duties and Hergé was free to focus on the work that mattered most to him.

He was happy with this development and relaxed into his role. *Cigars of the Pharaoh* had just received glowing reviews, and this spurred Hergé on to write his next adventure – but Tintin would not be called up.

Hergé wanted to try out something new for *Le Petit Vingtième*, and his next tale would be *The Adventures of Popol and Virginia in the Far West*, eventually shortened to *Popol out West*, which served as a rest for the artist from the constraints of the Tintin model.

However, although Hergé wanted a break, his fans did not and the newspaper started to receive letters of complaint. Tintin came back to the pages of *Le Petit Vingtième* sharpish to announce the next instalment, which would be *The Blue Lotus*, the second half of the *Tintin in the Orient* story that Hergé had begun with *Cigars of the Pharaoh*. Tintin appeared in March on the cover of *Le Petit Vingtième* exclaiming, 'Hello, Brussels? This is Rawhajpoutalah.'

Inside the paper he explains he is not yet ready to relax into retirement – he has more scoundrels to catch and this time, the group are in the Far East. He is asked by the staff, 'Aren't you afraid of the Chinese, Tintin?'

He replies with, 'Afraid of the Chinese? There are all different kinds of them, of course, like the Europeans. But the Chinese are generally very charming people; polite, very sophisticated, and hospitable. Many of the missionaries I've met on my travels have spoken of their love for China.' He ends with, 'It would be wrong to believe that all Chinese people are liars, or cruel, etc.'

Up to that point, Hergé had not portrayed the Chinese particularly sympathetically. In *Tintin in the Land of the Soviets* he had featured two barbaric Chinese men with pigtails hired by the Soviets to torture Tintin. Later on, in *Tintin in America*, he added two Chinese thugs who planned to kill and eat Snowy.

So Tintin's comments in this fictional interview marked a sharp about-turn for the artist and were relatively liberal for the time, a sign of Hergé's growing maturity. He had also received a message from Father Léon Gosset, who was a chaplain to the Chinese students at the University of Louvain. Gosset had urged him to be sensitive in his work on China, given previous comic strips he had produced. He told Hergé that his students were avid fans of the Tintin series and would be upset if he were to use crude stereotypes of their country.

Hergé arranged a meeting with Gosset, who in turn put the artist in contact with a few of his charges, including Arnold Chiao Ch'eng-Chih and his wife, Susan Lin. After speaking to the couple, Hergé wrote to the third student, Zhang Chong Ren for the first time on 30 March, which would turn out to be a pivotal moment in the artist's life.

At this point, Hergé was seeking inspiration and advice from many people and he was very receptive to the opinions of others, particularly those from the Catholic sphere and the newspaper. He once again spoke to the figure he had met during a Scouting camp years earlier, the same man who had advised him on his relationship with Germaine: Father Edouard Neut.

Neut had a special interest in China and he was currently working for Father Dom Lou Tseng Tsiang, a former prime minister of China, who had become a monk after the death of his wife. Hergé asked Father Neut for his opinion on his new ideas for Tintin, and Neut replied positively to the letter saying that a by-product of this work would be to introduce Tintin to people in the Far East, and it should also serve to increase understanding and, hopefully, friendship between the different races.

To aid Hergé's research, Father Neut posted him two books – *On the Origins of the Manchu Conflict* by Father Thadee and *My Mother* by Zheng, the latter to give an idea of family life in China.

Hergé wrote back to thank Father Neut and told him how much he had learned so far. He had found out that Chinese people living in Belgium were very often shocked at the way people discussed their country and Hergé realised how biased and wrong his own attitude had previously been.

The young cartoonist spent a great deal of time learning about the different culture and found himself developing a sympathy and true admiration for the Chinese, along with a much deeper understanding. From these experiences, he felt very strongly that the pervasive attitudes regarding China and the Chinese needed to be changed in Belgium, particularly in children, which is where he could make an impression – and he was determined to do so.

Hergé had not been overly concerned with depicting other cultures accurately before, and he had never bothered himself too much about research, having been generally content to rely on laboured and racist stereotypes up until this point (think *Tintin in the Congo, Tintin in the Land of the Soviets* and *Tintin in America*).

So, what had caused this sudden change in style? Just two weeks before his letter to Father Neut, on Sunday, 1 May 1934, Hergé met with Zhang Chong Ren for the first time. Zhang appeared at Hergé's apartment at 5 pm sharp and that meeting would change the course of history for Hergé.

Zhang was 26 years old, just a year younger than Hergé, and made an indelible impression on the artist from the first moment. He was originally from Shanghai and his family were artists. He had studied at the École Saint-Louis and was fluent in French. While he had toyed with the idea of being an actor in his youth, in 1931 he received a scholarship to study painting and sculpture at the Royal Academy of Beaux-Arts in Brussels, and didn't look back.

Hergé and Zhang had a great deal in common and Hergé found the artist fascinating. They became firm friends and after that very first visit, Zhang would spend every Sunday afternoon with Hergé for over a year. Although Zhang was younger, the cartoonist felt he had much to learn from him and adopted the young man as his next mentor.

It was from Zhang that Hergé developed a sense of world politics, but also a sense of responsibility with his art, as well as new drawing styles. This was a major turning point for Hergé, and he would later say: 'Zhang was, without knowing it, one of the principal influences on my evolution.'

One Sunday, Zhang gave Hergé a set of traditional Chinese paintbrushes along with an instruction book for a linear drawing style. He demonstrated different techniques, showing Hergé how to paint with feeling, from showing the softness of petals and the hardness of rocks, to capturing nature with accuracy and movement. Zhang also taught Hergé about Chinese calligraphy, as well as explaining the principles of Taoist philosophy. The training Zhang offered had a profound effect on Hergé who had not been exposed to any of these things until now.

All of these influences contributed to Hergé's growth during the period in which he created *The Blue Lotus*, and while he continued to meet with the first Chinese students he had been introduced to, Zhang played a special part in his development, shown by the fact that Zhang was made into a fictional character in the Tintin series. Indeed, he first appeared in *The Blue Lotus* as a young orphan whom Tintin saved from drowning.

The Blue Lotus carries on the story from the previous adventure, *Cigars of the Pharaoh*. Tintin and Snowy are invited to China, but they arrive to find themselves in the middle of the 1931 Japanese invasion. Here the crime-solving duo uncover a network of Japanese spies and another drug smuggling ring.

This new Tintin adventure marks a change of direction for Hergé again, an evolution in terms of style and technique, but also in terms of the narrative. He focuses on real events and is keen to show his readers what he believes is an accurate version of what is happening in the world at that very moment, as influenced by his new friend, Zhang, who was highly critical of the Japanese army.

In *The Blue Lotus*, Tintin has a new awareness and attitude to different cultures. When he stops Mr Gibbons beating a rickshaw driver with his cane, the man then goes and complains to his cohorts: 'Keeping me from beating a Chink! Intolerable, isn't it? What is the world coming to if we can't even teach these dirty Yellows a thing or two about politeness?'

This language is shocking today, but by showing Tintin as someone who would stand up for the Chinese, Hergé sent out a clear anti-racism message, which was revolutionary at this time in Belgium and directly contrasted with the other comic strips in the country.

In addition to this new-found sensitivity, there is a highly charged political awareness to this Tintin story. Before meeting Zhang, Hergé knew very little of the events happening in China but through Zhang's vivid and impassioned descriptions, Hergé had one side of the story and translated this straight into the pages of *Le Petit Vingtième*.

At the time, China was in conflict. The country was embroiled in a devastating civil war and also engaged in a vicious battle with the invading Japanese army. Zhang was particularly upset at the incident in Mukden, an event staged by the Japanese military as a pretext for the Japanese invasion of Manchuria. On 18 September 1931, the army had orchestrated a small explosion close to a railway line owned by Japan's South Manchuria Railway near Mukden. The explosion itself had had little effect on the railway lines and a train passed over the track unharmed soon after, but the Imperial Japanese Army immediately accused Chinese dissidents of the act and then responded with a full invasion leading to the occupation of Manchuria.

Zhang was incensed and after discussions with Hergé, they decided to include the attack in the Tintin story to raise awareness of the current problems in China. Hergé used *The Blue Lotus* to explore the prevailing attitudes of the time, with Tintin at one point giving a speech to Chang explaining Western misunderstandings of the Chinese. He also criticised Western activity in China's International Settlement by depicting it as corrupt, which was highly controversial.

Much of the information used for the adventure was from Zhang, who naturally gave his own perspective. One criticism of the story is that is does not contain a balanced view – the Long March of Communist Mao Zedong does not even get a mention.

Even though he only approached the subject with one side of the story, Hergé wanted to portray complete accuracy so he started to use photographs to copy from. He would use these to draw Chinese clothing, street scenes and landscapes. His new penchant for realism would continue in the rest of Tintin's adventures. However, this accuracy extended even to the Chinese street signs, which boldly displayed political slogans translated as 'Down with Imperialism', 'Abolish unfair treaties', and 'Down with Japanese merchandise'.

The cartoonist seems to have gone from expounding racist propaganda for Abbot Wallez to expounding racist propaganda for Zhang. While the Chinese students in Belgium were thrilled with this new development and became a firm fan base, the Japanese diplomats were up in arms about the whole affair and sent an official complaint to the newspaper.

Hergé was concerned about the trajectory this story was taking, but Zhang urged him to stay strong in the face of this pressure. He said, 'Don't be afraid! If the Japanese are angry it's because we're telling the truth. Tell your editor that Belgium is a free country. So Japan is threatening to prosecute us before the International Court of Justice in The Hague? All the better! It's not as if you're spreading lies. Everything you show in *The Blue Lotus* is taken from actual events. So everyone will know the truth – and you'll be world famous!'

The story was another commercial success, and *Le Petit Vingtième* organised a flamboyant event to celebrate 'the return of Tintin from the Far East', sponsored this time by the L'Innovation and Bon Marché department stores. The paper again organised an actor to play Tintin, as well as a contortionist and a clown. The event was held at the Cirque Royal with 3,000 fans flooding to the area, many of whom were again from Scouting groups.

In September 1935, Hergé was dealt another blow – Zhang's family had requested he return home to China. Hergé was smitten with Zhang and distraught at the thought of losing his close friend. Hergé went to the station to say goodbye, but just missed Zhang, who recalls boarding the train and looking out of the window for his friend. Eventually he saw Hergé appear and chase after the train waving his handkerchief.

Hergé dealt with the loss by throwing himself into his work and continuing in the practices his great friend had taught him. He focused on arranging the latest comic strips into book format, and then approached his publisher with a list of suggestions. He wanted Casterman to be more aggressive with this story and asked for better placement in bookshops, showing his business and commercial acumen.

At that moment, the story was still called *Tintin in the Far East*, and Charles Lesne wanted Hergé to find a more exciting title and also proposed a major new development: the addition of colour. For the title, Hergé suggested *The Blue Lotus* because it was short, and it sounded Chinese, mysterious and exotic. First and foremost, Hergé wanted complete colour in the book, but as that was not possible, they settled for a few coloured fold-out sections, which Hergé started to work on alongside his work for the cover.

The cover is also a change of direction for the artist and features Tintin hiding in a pot with a mural of a Chinese dragon behind him. This marks the beginning of a more artistic style for the Tintin series.

While he waited for the book to be published, which wouldn't be until October 1936, Hergé worked on the next Tintin adventure, which started in December 1935 and took his hero to a different part of the world.

Chapter 5

This time the adventure begins at a museum in Brussels, where a South American fetish, which has the eponymous broken ear, is stolen. Tintin and Snowy chase the thieves to the fictional country of San Theodoros, where the pair become caught up in a bitter war, and also find the Arumbaya tribe hidden away in the forest.

The most tightly scripted story in the series so far, Hergé uses a combination of his trademark fast-paced storyline and a new-found political awareness to great effect. Indeed, after the influence of Zhang on *The Blue Lotus*, current affairs were never too far away from Hergé's stories. Hergé now saw the world and politics in a whole new light and sought to include these matters in his work more and more.

In *The Broken Ear*, Hergé uses the Chaco War for inspiration, which was fought between Bolivia and Paraguay in the period 1932 to 1935. They were fighting over control of the northern part of the Gran Chaco region of South America, thought to be rich in oil. Hergé read the satirical French magazine *Le Crapouillot* avidly and used the details of the conflict in his storyline.

Bazarov, the gunrunner in the story, was inspired by Sir Basil Zaharoff, one of the most notorious criminals of the time. Zaharoff was a Greek arms dealer and industrialist and became one of the richest men in the world from these nefarious activities. He was described as a 'merchant of death' and 'mystery man of Europe', often using aggressive tactics in his dealings, including selling arms to opposing sides in conflicts, as Bazarov did in *The Broken Ear*.

Hergé enjoyed adding this sense of authenticity to his work, but found creating the complex story gruelling and confusing. He said, 'I didn't know anymore how to extricate myself. The story about the jewels – who was the killer? Who was the thief? Why? How? I couldn't figure it out any more.'

It was this complicated story that inspired Hergé to start a notebook with ideas, details, drawings and speech which would help him form a more cohesive narrative. He was beginning to hone his craft and focus on the story elements. While before he was thinking in terms of weekly comic strips, now he had the arc of the entire book at the forefront of his mind.

These notebooks were an important tool for Hergé, as his workload was increasing year on year and he was beginning to find it difficult to cope. In 1935, he was working harder than ever, taking little time to relax and this chronic overwork soon came back to haunt him as he became ill and suffered a depressive crisis.

When Hergé came up against difficult periods in his life, he would look for help from the same familiar faces. Rather than seeking comfort from his wife or parents or even friends his own age, in May he retreated to visit his former boss and mentor Abbot Wallez in his monastery in Aulne, leaving Germaine behind at home. His father sent him a letter saying he hoped the trip would provide a healthy break for him, allowing him to settle his nerves. But Hergé couldn't rest and he continued to draw in Aulne at breakneck speed, and soon returned home to continue the same stressful lifestyle.

He lasted a few more months before struggling again, and returned to visit the Abbot in August, once again feeling burnt out from overwork.

At this time, he was asked to provide a new comic strip for the French weekly *Coeurs Vaillants* (Valiant Hearts) which resulted in *The Adventures of Jo, Zette, and Jocko*, a series Hergé was not enamoured with, but was keen to do as he knew it would raise the profile of his other work in France.

He complained to Charles Lesne, the Casterman editor, about his increased workload. Hergé was now creating three stories a week, each of which took him around two days to complete. He was feeling overwhelmed and very aware that he couldn't take a break for any reason – illness or as he joked, imprisonment or 'a brick dropping on his head', and said that Lesne would be the death of him.

It was indeed too much for Hergé, and he soon dropped some of the illustration work so he could focus on his main projects.

He continued with *The Adventures of Jo, Zette, and Jocko* but he found that particular comic strip rather dull. The churchmen from the *Coeurs Vaillants* had asked him to include the characters' families to make this a more wholesome kind of adventure – but for Hergé, families had no place in his stories.

He said, 'They bored me terribly, these parents who wept all the time as they searched for their children who had gone off in all directions. These characters didn't have the total freedom enjoyed by Tintin.' He added, 'Think of Jules Renard's phrase: "Not everyone can be an orphan!" How lucky for Tintin – he is an orphan, and so he is free.' For Hergé, parents just got in the way, and in any case, he had more important things to be getting on with, such as the next Tintin adventure…

The Black Island, one of the most popular of the entire Tintin series, began in *Le Petit Vingtième* on 15 April 1937 and revolved around a band of counterfeiters, once again based on real events. Counterfeit money was becoming more and more of a problem, partly due to new technological developments, and Hergé was keen to reflect the situation of the time in his comic strip.

For this detective adventure, Tintin and Snowy travel to the UK, hot on the heels of a gang of counterfeiters. On their travels, the pair take in various Sussex sights including Newhaven and Seaford. While they are exploring, the pair are framed for theft, and Thomson and Thompson, incompetent detectives extraordinaire, arrive to capture them. Tintin and Snowy follow the real criminals to the Black Island off the coast of Scotland, where they happen upon their lair.

In March 1937 Hergé had visited the UK to gather information for this story and travelled widely around London and the south coast of England, but skipped Scotland. These travels, and the tales he encountered along the way of the Loch Ness monster, greatly influenced him for this story, as did various films, such as Hitchcock's *The 39 Steps* and the 1933 *King Kong* film.

Although he loved his trip to the UK and enjoyed creating the story, he found his workload overwhelming. Germaine said, 'He was always working, even on the weekends. He worked at night, on Saturday and Sunday, on Christmas, New Year's, Easter. What else could he do? He was doing Tintin, Quick and Flupke, Jo and Zette, and all those advertisements. He didn't get much rest.'

Certainly, life was all about the job for Hergé. While he would have certain friends over to his home, such as Paul Jamin or Philippe Gerard, they were people he knew from work and often they came by to chat about story ideas. Germaine, too, was a huge source of help and the main collaborator with Hergé. She would often assist with jokes, draw the lines that bordered the panels, add shading and retouch drawings. But with all his close friends and family associated with work, this meant there was little respite for Hergé.

Germaine and her husband rarely went out together. Germaine said, 'He didn't like to go to the theatre or the cinema, because he felt like that was watching something he did himself.' They would occasionally go on short trips away together to Coq-sur-Mer on the coast of Belgium, where they would stay at the Joli-Bois Hotel.

He was also friends with Marcel Dehaye, who he met through a group of artists he had been introduced to by an old colleague from *Le Petit Vingtième*. Other than that, he was a solitary figure with few close friends. He missed Zhang after he returned to China, and he would occasionally visit his former mentor Abbot Wallez, who was still away in Aulne, to seek help and guidance. Father Neut would sometimes visit Hergé and Germaine, and the cartoonist was grateful for his care and attention, something he felt his life generally lacked.

Hergé held a huge passion for nature and he would try to unwind by going for long walks when he had time, but Germaine was concerned about him. She worried about his habit of overworking himself and she was also anxious about his health, later saying, 'It wasn't that he was really sick, but he always had liver trouble, which made him tired.' They had a strong relationship, but had very different personalities and lived a fairly isolated existence together, and they would only rarely see family.

Work preoccupied Hergé and gave him a purpose, as well as an increasingly large source of income. In 1938 he bought his first car – an Opel Olympia – which was his pride and joy. He loved the car so much he planned on featuring it in the next Tintin adventure.

With his success, he started to think even more commercially, laying out plans for Hergé Studios and a focus on bookshops dedicated to Tintin, plans that seemed unattainable at the time, but would one day come to fruition.

By the late 1930s the world was in turmoil as Hitler posed an ever more ominous threat. King Leopold III had begged for a neutral stance for Belgium, urging his ministers to focus on keeping the war away from their territory, rather than preparing for war as part of a coalition. He wanted the interests of Belgium and its people to be put first above all else.

On 11 March 1938, German troops invaded Austria, with Hitler announcing the country was now part of the Third Reich. In September, the Nazis invaded Czechoslovakia, and Hergé was concerned about being called up for military service but was passed over, and free to continue work on his latest comic strip.

Hergé was now focusing his efforts on a new story entitled *The Adventures of Tintin in Syldavia*, now known as *King Ottokar's Sceptre*, which drew heavily from current events.

In this adventure Tintin and Snowy travel to the fictional Balkan nation of Syldavia. Here they discover a plot to overthrow King Muskar XII, and cunningly manage to foil the criminals. The story began in *Le Petit Vingtième* on 4 August 1938 and finished just over a year later on 10 August 1939, three weeks before Germany invaded Poland, when the Belgians were increasingly worried about their own position and the threat of Nazi invasion.

By 1939, as the Italians invaded Albania, Hergé spoke to his publisher to urge him to publish the story in book form as soon as possible to cash in on the topical nature of his latest work. Hergé said to his editor, Charles Lesne, 'If you've read the story at all you know it's completely based on current events. Syldavia is Albania. It's preparing to be annexed. If we want to take advantage of its topicality, it's now or never.' The book was released that November.

Hergé had created a satirical version of Nazi Germany called Borduria, naming the leader of the country 'Müsstler', a fusion of 'Hitler' and 'Mussolini'. The Bordurian officers wore uniforms similar in style to the uniforms of the German SS, and even the Bordurian planes were based on German designs.

In Syldavia, Hergé used a variety of Eastern European countries as inspiration, but predominantly based the satirical country on Albania, with the black pelican of the Syldavian flag echoing the black eagle of Albania's. Syldavia was also a symbol of Belgium, and illustrated the fear felt by the Belgians, with Syldavian King Muskar XII bearing more than a slight resemblance to Belgium's King Leopold III.

This book introduced a range of new characters in the shape of Hector and Alfred Alembick, as well as the famous 'Milanese Nightingale' Bianca Castafiore, based on opera singer Maria Callas, who would appear in more Tintin stories in the future and become a firm fan-favourite.

In this story, Hergé employed a neat device to give the reader information about the country of Syldavia without slowing the story. At the time Tintin discovers a tourist pamphlet about Syldavia in the adventure, Hergé inserted the very same pamphlet that Tintin reads into the book – a feature that the fans loved.

The latest adventure was well received and readers enjoyed the cutting political satire, the tightly plotted storyline, as well as the Hitchcockian style full of drama and comedy. Indeed, this instalment showed a more mature side of Hergé and was a huge commercial success, leading Hergé to start thinking about his next story.

One day, while he had been busy creating *King Ottokar's Sceptre*, he had taken his Siamese cat for one of the long walks that he would often go on. He happened upon a four-storey house a few kilometres from the city, set on the edge of a forest, and was smitten. He and Germaine made the decision to leave the bright lights of Brussels behind them, and on 15 May 1939 the couple bought the house and moved into their new home. With a large balcony and being set so near a park, it offered a serene sanctuary from the hectic world that surrounded them and their busy lifestyles. They relished the retreat and the space their new house gave them, but it was just a few months later that Hergé was jolted out of his idyllic hideaway.

On 1 September 1939, Germany, under the command of Hitler, invaded Poland and just two days later, England and France declared war on Germany. Hergé was called up to the army as Belgium struggled with the situation. Hubert Pierlot was the leader of the government and they tried to keep as neutral a stance as possible. King Leopold III took control of the army.

Hergé was sent to the tiny village of Herenthout by mistake with a large group of soldiers, where they passed the time in a cafe with Hergé writing reams of letters, mainly to Germaine. He was temporarily demobilised a couple of weeks after arriving and was happy to return to work on Tintin. Indeed, on 28 September, the cover of *Le Petit Vingtième* proudly proclaimed 'Tintin is back' with a big picture of Tintin in a military uniform, and showing his order of demobilisation – Hergé was ready to work.

Land of Black Gold began on 12 October 1939, with the plot revolving around Tintin's attempts to find the militant group responsible for sabotaging oil supplies in the Middle East, inspired by a story in *Le Crapouillot* magazine. Hergé continued with his comic strip each week, despite the war raging in the countries around Belgium and the threat of invasion looming over them.

In this new adventure, Hergé brought back many of the favourite characters from previous stories, such as Dr Müller, a German villain from *The Black Island*, the Portuguese merchant Oliveira da Figueira from *Cigars of the Pharaoh*, and he also mentioned the larger-than-life Bianca Castafiore.

New characters also appeared in the shape of the Emir Ben Kalish Ezab, a character who was loosely based on Ibn Saud, the king of Saudi Arabia, and Iraqi leader, Faisal I, while other fictionalised Arabic names dotted throughout the story offered a play on words in Marollien, a Brussels dialect, such as 'Bab El Ehr', which was Marollien for 'chatterbox'.

Hergé continued with his work when in December of 1939, he received a letter from Father Neut detailing a telegram he had received from China inviting Hergé to visit with all costs paid. The telegram was from Madame Tchang and Mr Tong, the minister of the Publicity Board. Tong apparently wanted Hergé to produce a weekly newspaper for children, as well as illustrations for the education department of the Chinese government.

Hergé was keen, despite serving in the current world war, and his contractual obligations with *Le Petit Vingtième*. He replied enthusiastically to Mr Tong, describing how he might be able to come if his stay wasn't too long and if he was able to do his drawings in advance of the trip for *Le Petit Vingtième*. He also says that Germaine would be able to add finishing touches to the drawings while he was away, showing the degree to which Germaine supported Hergé and how much he trusted her professionally.

However, this collaboration with the Chinese government didn't happen, and Hergé was called back to the army on 28 December and served as a lieutenant in the city of Antwerp.

As well as his duties in the army, Hergé was determined to continue drawing the Tintin strip, but he was only able to produce a page per week. A lack of time meant he had been forced to stop all the other work, too – no more *Quick and Flupke* or *Jo, Zette and Jocko*.

But he had friends in high places. Charles du Bus de Warnaffe, the former Belgian Minister of Justice, stepped in and insisted Hergé was given two days off military duty per week to work on Tintin.

Despite the special treatment allowing him time off from his military service, Hergé was struggling. He was becoming ill with overwork and stress, and complained that a February issue of *Le Petit Vingtième* had given him 'terrible sinusitis'.

He also developed an attack of boils, which would be a recurring problem for him, especially at stressful times, and he was given leave to return home on 17 April, again on a temporary basis. He wrote a letter to his readers to apologise for missing an instalment of Tintin:

> '*My dear little friends of Le Petit Vingtième,*
>
> *Due to extraordinary circumstances (!), I have been unable to give you the next instalment of the adventures of our friends Tintin and Milou (Snowy) this week. I beg your pardon very humbly.*
>
> *And I promise you that, barring unforeseen circumstances (earthquake, tidal wave, tornado, or bombardment), you will be reunited with our two heroes and the ever-present police in next Thursday's issue.*'

Hergé continued to struggle with health problems, and in May he was declared unfit for service. This exempted him from military duty and meant he could return home permanently.

On 10 May 1940, Hitler launched an attack against Belgium, the Netherlands and Luxembourg. *Le Vingtième Siècle*, which was already struggling, folded and the staff dispersed.

The Germans attacked Belgium with tanks and planes, and after just two days had overcome the defences that protected access to Brussels. The capital would soon be occupied. The former editor of *Le Vingtième*

Siècle told Hergé to leave the city as soon as possible, and so Hergé and Germaine packed up their Opel Olympia and fled with their Siamese cat, Thaïke, Hergé's sister-in-law, Jeannot, and their three-year-old niece, Denise.

They hurried to gather only their most precious belongings and drove south, instinctively heading to meet one of Hergé's long-time mentors, Father Neut. They arrived at Lophem in the afternoon, where they were met by the familiar faces of Father Neut and Father Lou. The latter was very taken with their cat, and was impressed that the pair had not abandoned the animal in their rush to leave the war-struck city. Hergé was touched and moved by the emotion Father Lou showed his pet, and would never forget the kindness he had given them.

The group arrived in Paris, and scoured the Latin Quarter looking for a hotel without any luck. Hergé bumped into a friend he had previously collaborated with, Marie-France Sebileau. She gave the group a place to stay and then told them to drive south where they would be able to stay with Marijac, a cartoonist.

They drove to Saint-Germain-Lembron only to find that Marijac had been called up to serve in the army, but his wife managed to find them a place to stay in a village a short distance away.

It was an extremely fearful time. Hergé's parents were stuck in Brussels and he was desperate to pass a message on to let them know that their little group were all safe. He wrote to his Portuguese publisher, asking them to send the message to his father.

He also asked for payment of the fees he was owed for *Tintin in the Congo* and *The Broken Ear*, as the group had left in haste and without many resources to keep them going. These fees would tide them over for a while, at least.

Politically, the situation in Belgium was falling apart. Major clashes between the government ministers and the king resulted in ministers fleeing to France, while the king refused to leave and continued to direct all the military operations. He wanted to keep Belgium as an independent country and was also keen to ensure the future of the monarchy.

But the attacks from the Germans were relentless. In eighteen days, the Germans had slaughtered 18,000 soldiers of the Belgian army. Hitler wanted an unconditional surrender and King Leopold III, without discussing the matter with their allies, eventually agreed so that the bloodshed would stop and to prevent further attacks against his men.

A ceasefire was announced at 4 am on 28 May. The French were shocked at his actions and even the Belgian ministers said that the king was unfit to reign. On that same day, King Leopold III broadcast a radio message saying: 'I am not leaving you in the adversity that is overwhelming us, and I will be here to watch over you and your families. Tomorrow we will go to work with the unwavering determination to help the country arise from its ruins anew.' He asked the Belgians who had fled to other countries to return home.

Hergé agreed with the king's decision, but for practical reasons remained in France until 28 June, when he learned that the road had been reopened. He and Germaine drove to Vichy that night, as they had been promised a supply of petrol from a friend who lived there, and then they drove on to Belgium as quickly as they could.

Arriving back in Brussels on 30 June, Hergé found Belgium was now occupied by the Nazis, and under the control of General Alexander von Falkenhausen, who was under strict orders to stabilise the country and use Belgium's resources as intensively as possible for the needs of the German war. The king was under house arrest in Laeken Castle, and the rest of the country tried to function under the Occupation.

After *Le Vingtième Siècle* and *Le Petit Vingtième* folded, Hergé was unemployed and was having real financial difficulty. There were attempts to restart *Le Vingtième Siècle*, but it was refused authorisation by the Germans. Hergé was in trouble.

Chapter 6

With no job, the situation was getting desperate for Hergé. He was offered a role on *Le Pays Reel*, a newspaper published by the Catholic-Fascist Rexist Party, to start at the end of August. Despite his precarious position he declined as, aside from not paying particularly well, he had concerns over the credibility of the newspaper, which would later prove to be a wise move. Jean Vermeire took the job instead.

Hergé decided to focus all his efforts on a *Quick and Flupke* anthology instead. While he was working on this, he received another offer, this one all the more tempting. *Le Soir*, formerly the main newspaper in Belgium, approached Hergé and asked him to help start up an illustrated children's weekly in the style of *Le Petit Vingtième*. It was 5 September and the team had everything ready to go; they just needed final authorisation, as all newspapers were now under the strict control of the Nazis, and in particular Von Falkenhausen.

Le Soir had been the biggest newspaper in Belgium for a long time and had a firmly established reputation and reader-base. The Rossel family owned *Le Soir*, but were no longer in Brussels and the paper had been impounded by the Germans. After talking to the team who wanted to revive the paper, the Germans authorised the project and allowed production to restart. However, they wanted the controversial Belgian journalist Raymond De Becker to manage the publication.

Hergé had reservations about the job. But it had a reputable name and an astronomical circulation – it was too good an opportunity to turn down, and he accepted.

The newspapers that restarted under the Nazi Occupation were called 'pirate' editions, and Hergé's decision to join the 'pirate' edition of *Le Soir* would later lead to the most difficult time of his life when he was accused of collaborating with the Nazis.

He would later say he felt that joining *Le Pays Reel* would have been a political act, but not working for *Le Soir*. He didn't feel as though he was collaborating and that wasn't his intention – he was just producing a children's supplement after all! The cartoonist just wanted to get back to work and, as a royalist, he felt he was following the king's instructions.

Hergé joined the team on 15 October and they spent months assembling the new version, before the first issue of the 'pirate' *Le Soir* was published on 13 June. The issue was a huge success, with the circulation rising swiftly from 60,000 to 200,000.

On 31 August, De Becker was named 'head of administrative and editorial services', and the Germans were happy with his progress, calling *Le Soir* the 'newspaper of national reconstruction'.

The ambitious De Becker, who was just 28 at the time he became director of *Le Soir*, had strong affinities with the Nazi party, and he seized the opportunity to try to implement changes in the political system.

De Becker followed guidelines from the 'Propaganda Abteilung', and gave detailed instructions to the *Le Soir* staff – the journalists could write whatever they wanted, but it had to conform to German wishes. While they should not write anything that opposed the ideas patronised by the Germans, they could occasionally abstain from defending a given idea from the Nazis – but not regularly or even often.

Hergé's role and level of involvement in the political side of the paper was ambiguous. He later admitted he was sure that Raymond De Becker had sympathised with the Nazis, and even confessed that he himself had believed the future of the West was in the hands of the New Order.

He felt that for many people democracy had proved deceptive, and the New Order brought fresh hope. This was a fairly common belief in Catholic circles, but Hergé regretted it deeply. He later said that given everything that happened, it was a terrible error to have believed, even for an instant, in the Nazi ideology.

During this time, his brother Paul, who was a soldier in the army, had been captured by the Germans and was sent to a prisoner of war camp in Germany.

Although Hergé's sympathies were sometimes ambiguous, those of the newspaper were not. There were announcements about the 'great speech by the Führer in Berlin', copy celebrating the feats of the German military, and Jewish people were often discussed in derogatory terms.

While working for *Le Soir*, Hergé met Jacques Van Melkebeke, another artist who would become a long-term collaborator of his. With Van Melkebeke, as well as Paul Jamin to assist him, Hergé soon managed to produce the *Soir-Jeunesse*, which was virtually a carbon copy of *Le Petit Vingtième*, and most importantly included a brand new Tintin adventure.

By 17 October 1940, when the new Tintin adventure started, the circulation of *Le Soir* was over 300,000 – a figure that dwarfed the circulation of the former *Le Vingtième Siècle*. As well as contributing two pages of the new Tintin adventure each week, Hergé illustrated the cover, titles and added other drawings. He also brought back *Quick and Flupke*, but it was the new Tintin adventure that captured the imagination of the readers.

The Crab with the Golden Claws tells the story of Tintin and Snowy's adventures in Morocco to capture a gang of international opium smugglers, and this instalment in the series is particularly important as we are first introduced to a character that would become an icon – the rambunctious Captain Haddock.

Hergé later said, 'I found an orphan by chance, born dead-drunk through no wish of his own, in a cabin of the Karaboudjian. I ended up loving him, and Tintin reeducated him.'

Captain Haddock was a major addition to the Tintin oeuvre and in many ways usurped Snowy as a central character. Snowy and Tintin had always had a very close relationship, and Snowy had until now been able to talk to humans, but after *The Crab with the Golden Claws*, he was no longer able to speak, showing just how much his role had diminished in the adventures.

With its exotic charm, dream sequences and influences from Hitchcockian thrillers, the story was a big hit and showed a new-found maturity in the characterisations.

However, the war would soon provide another obstacle for the series – a lack of paper. Due to the shortage, in May 1941 the directors changed the format of the comic strip. To begin with, it was reduced by a third, then reduced further to daily 17cm by 4cm strips, which meant that planning became a crucial part of the process for Hergé and he could no longer improvise as much as he had before.

Hergé rose to the challenge and created one of the greatest adventures yet for his readers, and Charles Lesne at Casterman was soon in touch asking to publish the next book in the series. The cartoonist had to reassure him that the changes to the format would not delay production.

At the same time, Hergé was increasingly frustrated by mistakes appearing in his books and asked to see proofs before they went to print, but this rarely happened. He wrote to Casterman often to complain, explaining that due to the technique involved, he really needed to see and approve all the frames. When he received the latest copy of his work from the publisher that he had not been allowed to proofread, he was by turns saddened and enraged by the results.

However, despite disagreements on the quality, the demand for the books had soared thanks to Hergé's work in *Le Soir* and the huge circulation it commanded, but the demand was such that Casterman could not keep up. At one point, Charles Lesne advised Hergé to suspend the planned advertising campaign for a few weeks as they were swamped with orders for *The Crab with the Golden Claws*; he was concerned that they would completely sell out and they didn't have enough paper for a reprinting at such short notice. The manufacturers simply could not keep up.

Due to the huge increase in demand, by December, it was confirmed that all of Hergé's books would be reprinted, and this was the start of great success for the cartoonist.

Meanwhile, at *Le Soir*, in August 1941, Raymond De Becker wrote and published a set of articles denouncing Communism and encouraging solidarity to unite Belgium and Europe against Russia. He also ventured into racist diatribes against the Jews.

In the current climate, Abbot Wallez found his views were en vogue again and he returned to politics very briefly to deliver a speech, before being chastised by his superiors and recalled back to the Aulne Abbey.

At the end of 1941, it was revealed that King Leopold III had married Lilian Baels, the daughter of a former government minister. This caused shockwaves throughout the country. Until this news, people had thought highly of the king who they assumed was mourning his beloved wife, Queen Astrid, who had been killed in a car crash on 29 August 1935, and believed he was suffering under house arrest alone.

Daily life in Belgium was hard – there was a lack of food and resources, and the citizens were struggling to get by. Hergé found a way around the food shortage by using his contacts abroad. His comic strips were featured in a Portugeuse newspaper, *Il Papagaio*, and he would ask the staff to send food parcels to him and also to his brother, who was still imprisoned in Germany. The newspaper would send luxuries such as chocolate, sugar, coffee, lard and cigarettes to the extremely grateful Hergé.

Other than a shortage of available luxuries, the cartoonist was relatively unaffected by the war at that time. He worked at home in Watermael-Boitsfort for twelve hours a day, occasionally travelling into the city to *Le Soir*'s offices. At this time, Hergé also branched out and wrote a play with Jacques Van Melkebeke, entitled *Tintin in the Indies* for the Theatre des Galeries. Hergé enjoyed the process immensely, and the play opened on 15 April 1941 to great success, with Tintin played by a woman named Jeanne Rubens, but Snowy proved trickier to organise. On the day the play opened, Van Melkebeke introduced Hergé to his childhood friend, Edgar Jacobs, who would become a very important figure in Hergé's life.

Hergé and Van Melkebeke wrote another play, entitled *Mr Boullock's Disappearance*, which opened again at the Theatre des Galeries over Christmas 1941 to a less than rapturous reception, but the cartoonist continued to advance into new areas. In the 1930s he had envisioned a range of spin-offs from the Tintin brand, and by July 1942 these would become a reality.

He also signed with an agent, Bernard Thiery, who took over business matters for Hergé. Each business project he managed, Thiery would take 40 per cent commission. *The Adventures of Tintin* were by now very successful, and the agent was keen to cash in on this. He asked Hergé to design postcards, colouring books and puzzles.

Hergé also occasionally illustrated for other writers, and had provided drawings for Robert de Vroylande's *Fables*, which was a less than wise move, as one of the tales in the book was highly anti-Semitic. The story was *Two Jews and Their Bet*, and Hergé's illustrations for the story included characters with anti-Semitic features – a decision he would later regret, as this was held up as the first clear piece of evidence often used against the cartoonist when he was accused of anti-Semitism.

This particular incident was followed by the next Tintin adventure, the tenth in the series, called *The Shooting Star* – another unfortunate mistake for Hergé, whose own star was rising at the time.

In this adventure, Tintin, Snowy and Captain Haddock set off on a scientific expedition to the North Pole in a race between two rival teams to find a meteorite, the 'Phostlite', that had fallen to Earth in a story that is widely believed to reveal Hergé's pro-Nazi and anti-Allied forces agenda.

The Shooting Star includes the United States as the main aggressors, and all of the scientists featured were from Axis, neutral, or occupied countries which many believed showed Hergé's bias. In December 1941, the Americans had just entered the war on the side of the Allies, and it was deeply contentious to have them featured in a comic strip in this way, and contributed to later accusations that Hergé faced of being a Nazi sympathiser.

Indeed, Hergé faced much criticism for this book, one of his most controversial, for using countries that were currently at war with each other as competing groups in the story, but most of all for the anti-Semitic portrayal of Jewish characters.

Perhaps the most damning part of the book is in the character named Blumenstein, a crooked financier who supports the American expedition, exhibiting all the typical anti-Semitic features of the time.

There were contentious parts of the story that featured in *Le Soir*, but were omitted from the book. One of them includes the scene where the prophet Philippulus announces the end of the world and bangs his gong. Two Jews have a conversation: 'Did you hear, Isaac? The end of the world! What if it's true?' The other replies: 'Hey, hey, it vould be a gut ding, Solomon! I owe my suppliers 50,000 francs, and zis way I von't haf to pay zem!'

Hergé denied any accusations of anti-Semitism or bias towards the Nazis, and it was thirty years after the book was published that he would admit that part of *The Shooting Star* concerned the rivalry for progress between Europe and the United States.

At the point the comic strip was published, Hergé's brother was still imprisoned in Germany, and according to one of Paul Remi's classmates, Albert Dellicour, who was imprisoned with him, Hergé's depictions in

The children's weekly, *Le Petit Vingtième*. (*Wikimedia Commons*)

The pre-Columbian statue that was the inspiration for the Arumbaya fetish in *The Broken Ear*. (*Vassil, Wikimedia Commons*)

The 'Gallery of Traitors' document. (*Brigade Piron, Wikimedia Commons*)

Île d'Or – the inspiration for *The Black Island*. (*Loïc Bigard, Wikimedia Commons*)

The magnificent Île d'Or. (*François Guinard / Wikimedia Commons / CC BY-SA 4.0*)

The house on Avenue Delleur in Brussels which was the inspiration for Professor Tarragon's house in *The Seven Crystal Balls*. (*Spirou et Fantasio, Wikimedia Commons*)

A display of Tintin books translated into different languages. (*Xavoun, Wikimedia Commons*)

A statue based on Hergé's characters. (*agracier - NO VIEWS, Wikimedia Commons*)

A mural of Tintin in Brussels. (*Ferran Cornellà, Wikimedia Commons*)

A sign on top of a building featuring Tintin and Snowy. (*C.Suthorn / cc-by-sa-4.0 / commons. wikimedia.org*)

Maria Callas - the inspiration for Milanese Nightingale, Bianca Castafiore. (*Joop van Bilsen / Anefo, Wikimedia Commons*)

Marlinspike Hall is modelled after the central section of the Château de Cheverny, a manor in France. (*werginz, Adobe Stock*)

Château de Cheverny. (*Laurent Renault, Adobe Stock*)

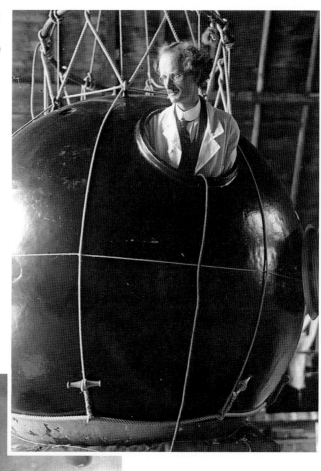

Auguste Piccard in one of his inventions. (*German Federal Archive, Wikimedia Commons*)

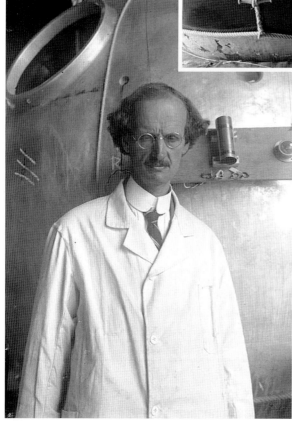

Auguste Piccard, Swiss physicist, inventor, explorer - and inspiration for Professor Cuthbert Calculus. (*German Federal Archive, Wikimedia Commons*)

The Emir's hideaway palace cut from the rock in *The Red Sea Sharks* was based on the Al Khazneh in Petra, Jordan. (*AJORON, Adobe Stock*)

Hergé's collaborator, Bob De Moor. (*ccbysa / GFDL, Wikimedia Commons*)

Statue of Hergé, with his cat and the characters of Tintin and Snowy, set near the Hergé Museum, in Louvain-La-Neuve, Belgium. (*Guy Delsaut, Wikimedia Commons*)

The Tintin rocket in Brussels Airport. (*Fawaz.tairou, Wikimedia Commons*)

The Hergé Museum, in Louvain-La-Neuve, near Brussels. (*Peripatetic, Wikimedia Commons*)

A train with Hergé's signature and Tintin in the window. (*Thalys, Wikimedia Commons*)

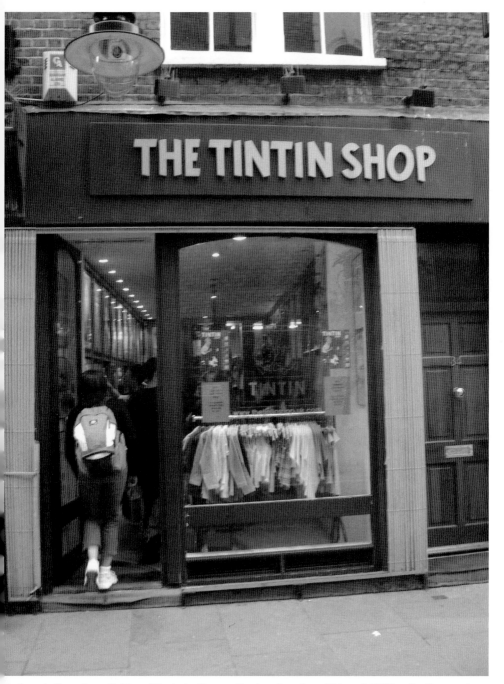

A shop dedicated to all things Tintin in Covent Garden, London. (*Edward, Wikimedia Commons*)

Tintin merchandise from *The Blue Lotus*. (*Thomas Quine, Wikimedia Commons*)

A Tintin-branded aeroplane. (*Wikimedia Commons*)

Tintin as an astronaut. (*Thomas Quine, Wikimedia Commons*)

Hergé's grave. (*Spirou et Fantasio, Wikimedia Commons*)

Spielberg and Tintin at the film premiere in Brussels, 2011. (*Georges Biard, Wikimedia Commons*)

Le Soir caused a great deal of anger in the prison camp. While reading the scene in the 'pirate' *Le Soir* with the boat full of 'bad guys' rowing toward the famous island and flying the American flag, Paul Remi turned green with rage. Other soldiers were also furious with Hergé's portrayal and what they deemed as his betrayal, and wrote angry letters, most of which would have been censored by the prison authorities and would not have reached Hergé.

After the war was over, when Hergé was accused of anti-Semitism, the argument he would use time and time again if challenged was that *The Shooting Star* was an old project, written before the existence of the Nazi extermination camps. He insisted that if it had been created later, he would not have introduced a character named Blumenstein to avoid any hint of racism. He pointed to the fact that there were many different caricatures in his work of many different unpleasant individuals, such as English colonists who mistreated the Chinese, German killers, double-dealing Japanese people and African witch-doctors, as well as gangsters from Chicago. He insisted that although he created caricatures of all these people, he had no ill-feeling against people of any race.

He would later say, 'All I actually did was show a villainous financier with a Semitic appearance and a Jewish name: Blumenstein, in *The Shooting Star*. But does that mean there was anti-Semitism on my part? It seems to me that in my entire panoply of bad guys there are all sorts; I have shown a lot of "villains" of various origins, without any particular treatment of this or that race… We've always told Jewish stories, Marseillaise stories, Scottish stories. But who could have predicted that the Jewish stories would end as we know now that they did, in the death camps of Treblinka and Auschwitz?'

Hergé insisted that he hadn't known about the Nazi death camps until 1945, and that if he had, it would have been impossible for him to accept them, even indirectly, by continuing to work for newspapers controlled by the Germans.

At the time *The Shooting Star* appeared in *Le Soir*, strong anti-Semitic rhetoric was appearing frequently in the news and comment pages. Leon Van Huffel wrote a piece in *Le Soir* declaring that it was no longer enough to exclude Jews from certain areas of control in public life. He said that they should consider Jewish people foreigners from an opposing race and 'refuse to mingle our blood with his'. He said that the time for social anti-Semitism is past and that all of Europe was now entering an era of racial anti-Semitism. The message of the newspaper was clear and unambiguous.

The Shooting Star finished in *Le Soir* on 27 May 1942 and a week later, the Jews in Belgium were ordered to wear the yellow star in order to identify themselves. Soon there were Gestapo raids and Jews were taken away and killed in Belgium.

Slowly, the full horror of what was happening unfolded and became apparent to everyone. Hergé said in 1974, 'I saw very few Jews wearing the yellow star, but finally I did see some. They told me some Jews were gone, that people had come for them and sent them away. I didn't want to believe it.'

After the war had ended, Hergé had the opportunity to change the story of *The Shooting Star* when a reprinting of the book was scheduled. He took this chance to change the flag of the US to the less contentious flag of the fictional country of Sao Rico. He also changed the name of the ruthless financier from Blumenstein to Bohlwinkel, intending this to be a play on words, based on the name for a little candy shop in the Brussels dialect, which was 'bollewinkel'. He insisted that he changed this to Bohlwinkel to make it sound more exotic. However, Bohlwinkel, it transpired, was also a Jewish surname.

He also had the opportunity to change the appearance of the Jewish characters to seem less anti-Semitic, but chose not to. All in all, it was a half-hearted attempt to make up for his mistakes during the German Occupation.

Meanwhile, with competition in France and Switzerland, sales of the Tintin books were decreasing due to the lack of colour. Louis Casterman, Hergé's publisher, visited him in March 1941 to try to persuade him to switch to a colour publication. Hergé was not keen, and strongly resisted.

In 1942, Lesne tried once again to persuade Hergé to consider using colour in his work and this time he was successful – the cartoonist finally gave in. They committed to revisiting all of the previous books and reissuing them as colour stories.

Hergé wanted Edgar Jacobs to collaborate with him, but Jacobs had other obligations and would not have enough time to devote to this task.

Instead, Hergé hired a young colourist and Germaine also played a crucial role in helping him with the redesigns that became necessary along with the shift to colour.

This project was a huge undertaking. The team would work on this throughout 1942 until 1947, and while this was being done, Hergé carried on creating the new adventures of Tintin. The book sales, still of black and white versions, were soaring, and there were high hopes of enormous success for the colour books. Hergé was happy with the work and everything was progressing well.

The war only impeded Hergé in one obvious way at this point – there was still a lack of paper. Casterman could not keep up with the demand and found themselves unable to provide the quantities of books that stores were asking for, but they were already thinking ahead to a time after the war had ended. They planned to have at least six or seven books ready to go in order to establish a firm presence in markets such as France and the Netherlands.

Casterman and Hergé were very aware that all publishers were in the same position – they were all preparing their new collections to launch as soon as possible once the war had finished, with everyone realising that the one who got there first would be in the best position to dominate the market.

Lesne wasn't content with just two or three books of the collection, as he thought the series would go unnoticed. He wanted to be able to have an entire set on the shelf. He knew how lucky they were to have such a popular series on their hands, and wanted to make the most of this with a prestigious launch as soon as the post-war period began. During the latter years of the war, Hergé, Germaine and his team worked flat out to prepare these books for the big launch.

Chapter 7

The colouring project continued in the background while Hergé concentrated on the task at hand – the latest adventure for Tintin, which would be in the form of a double book, encompassing *The Secret of the Unicorn* and *Red Rackham's Treasure*. After the disaster of *The Shooting Star*, he was careful to choose more neutral themes, and this time focused on a search for treasure.

In this benign story, Hergé could concentrate on completing his roll-call of characters in the Tintin series and flesh out the world they inhabited. The length of the book gave him the freedom and space to do this. For this adventure, Tintin, Snowy and Haddock discover a riddle left by one of Haddock's seventeenth-century ancestors, Sir Francis Haddock, which offers to lead them to the treasure left behind by the pirate Red Rackham. In order to solve the riddle, they must search for the three models of Sir Francis's ship, the *Unicorn*. However, a criminal network is also searching for the ship, and they have to defeat them.

Although Hergé had used various contributors from time to time, this is the first story where Jacques Van Melkebeke acted as a co-scriptwriter. Van Melkebeke had always been a voracious reader, devouring literature from Jules Verne and many others, and these influences are clear in this story. Van Melkebeke added many of the cultural references and biblical allusions that were scattered throughout *The Secret of the Unicorn*, as well as the scene in which Haddock relives the actions of his ancestors.

Hergé, inspired by his friend and collaborator, wanted to make his plots more complex in their structure, and they worked together to add depth to the adventure. Hergé was also intent on making elements of the story as realistic as possible, and when creating the old vessels, he sought help from a friend of his, Gérard Liger-Belair, who owned a shop in Brussels which specialised in model ships. Liger-Belair found plans of a seventeenth-century French warship for Hergé to use, called *Le Brillant*, constructed in 1690, which Hergé and his team meticulously copied.

The character of Red Rackham was based on the pirate Jack Rackham, also known as Calico Jack, who sailed with the female pirates Anne Bonny and Mary Read. It is in *The Secret of the Unicorn* that Marlinspike Hall, or Moulinsart in French, appears for the first time. The name comes from the Belgian town Sart-Moulin, while the design of the imposing mansion was based on the Château de Cheverny in the Loire Valley of France.

In this story, Sir Francis Haddock is introduced, making Captain Haddock the only character in the series so far to have a family, background and an ancestry. Hergé also alluded to the rumours surrounding his mysterious grandfather in making Francis Haddock a son of Louis XIV.

All the hard work paid off. The comic strip was another big hit and the books were selling extremely well – the first printing of *The Secret of the Unicorn* sold 30,000 copies. Perhaps most importantly, Hergé was happy with the story and it was his favourite of the Tintin adventures so far.

The Secret of the Unicorn finished in *Le Soir* on 14 January 1943, with *Red Rackham's Treasure* beginning soon after on 19 February. The Casterman publisher, Charles Lesne, was impressed with the speed and quality of the work, and was trying to keep up with demand from the book sales. However, he was not a fan of the pirate edition of *Le Soir*, and refused to read it, asking Hergé to send him the comic strips instead.

Red Rackham's Treasure completes the story arc that began with *The Secret of the Unicorn*, telling the tale of Tintin and Captain Haddock's trip to the Caribbean to search for Red Rackham's treasure.

In this tale the full family of characters are in place, which includes the addition of Professor Calculus, who would become a recurring character. Hergé had created many scientists and professors in earlier stories, such as Sophocles Sarcophagus in *Cigars of the Pharaoh*, Hector Alembick in *King Ottokar's Sceptre*, and Decimus Phostle in *The Shooting Star*, but in Calculus, Hergé had found the professor he had wanted for the Tintin series.

Hergé drew inspiration for Professor Calculus from a curious real-life character. He had been collecting press cuttings for years on the Swiss inventor Auguste Piccard, who had 'the furious ambition to rise ever higher into the sky and dive ever deeper in the ocean.'

Indeed, Piccard had been the first man to explore the stratosphere in a hot air balloon in 1931. Hergé added the comic deafness of the character, inspired by a former colleague of his from *Le Vingtième Siècle*. The eccentric professor was the perfect addition.

Hergé continued in his quest for realism within the confines of the comic strip. He and his team spent a great deal of time looking through newspaper clippings and archives for the right material for the latest story. Calculus's shark-shaped submarine was based on a real American submarine which Hergé had seen in a German newspaper, and the diving suit in the story was also based on clippings that Hergé had accumulated.

The tribal effigy Sir Francis Haddock found on a Caribbean island was based on a Bamileke tribal statue from Cameroon that Hergé had seen in a museum, and The Sirius was named after the SS *Sirius*, the first ship to cross the Atlantic Ocean solely under steam power. Even the brief appearance of Dr Daumière, who warns Haddock to cease drinking alcohol, was a nod to Hergé's own GP of the same name.

In this adventure, Tintin, who shifted his profession from reporter to the less contentious job of an explorer, a good move given the current political situation, was also shown wearing a white shirt under a blue sweater, which would become his iconic outfit. The trio of Tintin, Captain Haddock and Professor Calculus also buy and move into Haddock's family estate – Moulinsart, also known as the famous Marlinspike Hall. Indeed, Calculus completes the family of four central, core characters alongside Tintin, Haddock and Snowy, and this story shows Hergé reach maturity in his art form.

Red Rackham's Treasure is the best-selling story in *The Adventures of Tintin*, and the double story of *The Secret of the Unicorn* and *Red Rackham's Treasure* is possibly the most successful of all Tintin's adventures.

While work on *Red Rackham's Treasure* carried on with Hergé seemingly oblivious to the war, in the offices of *Le Soir* there were a few significant changes. Raymond De Becker flip-flopped his allegiances with various parties that were vying for power within Belgium, and the newspaper was shrinking little by little due to the ongoing paper shortages.

Soon, the Nazi war effort began to unravel. In Italy, Mussolini's regime fell on 3 September 1943, and it was widely thought that the defeat of the Germans would be imminent.

Raymond De Becker called a meeting with the writers, explaining that it was becoming less likely there would be a German victory, and that they should be vigilant concerning German propaganda. De Becker sent the speech he made to a group of high-ranking people, as well as the German embassy. Unsurprisingly, he was forced to resign his position as editor-in-chief, and was placed under house arrest by the Germans in the Bavarian Alps.

Hergé was loyal to De Becker, but was not moved to quit *Le Soir* in sympathy. He stayed on, contributing his comic strips while the paper resumed under the new editor-in-chief, Max Hodeige. The cartoonist was finishing *Red Rackham's Treasure* at the time, and would soon move on to the next adventure, *The Seven Crystal Balls*.

Hergé felt removed from the situation because he didn't feel that the war had anything to do with him, and in any case, he hated the Resistance movement. He was asked several times to join their group, but he refused as he felt it was contrary to the laws of war. Hergé would later say that for every one of the Resistance's actions, hostages would be arrested and shot, and he had wanted no part in their work.

All his time was spent on his comic strips, and he focused on his own career exclusively, with little thought of the war. His Casterman publishers disapproved of the pirate version of *Le Soir* and its collaborationist leanings. In September 1943, Charles Lesne wrote to Hergé after learning that *The Shooting Star* would be appearing in a Flemish-speaking newspaper *Het Laatste Nieuws* ('The Latest News').

Lesne was worried about Hergé's choices, and subtly suggested it would be better to wait for the end of the war before contributing to more newspapers. He said that while the war and the hostilities continued, it would be wise to hold back, as once the war was over, the reaction might not be very favourable. Lesne was concerned about the cartoonist, and although he phrased his questions delicately, Casterman were clearly worried about how Hergé's continued collaboration with pirate publications would be perceived in the post-war period.

Hergé appreciated Lesne's concern regarding the publication in *Het Laatste Nieuws*, but assured his publisher that he had thought long and hard about the decision, and he felt it was right to accept the offer from the Flemish newspaper.

He wanted to gain a foothold in as many publications as possible, even if the newspapers disappeared or changed direction after the war. Whatever happened afterwards, he said he was happy to have reached a larger group of the public, which was an excellent result for both of them.

Hergé realised that the reaction from the public for publishing in these pirate editions could be quite negative. He wrote: 'The reactions you fear are entirely possible. I would even say they're probable. There are unequivocal indications of that. But I'm already considered a 'traitor' for having published my drawings in *Le Soir*, for which I should be shot or hung (people haven't quite made up their minds about which one yet). The worst that can happen to me is that, having been shot (or hung) for my collaboration with *Le Soir*, I will be re-shot (or re-hung) for my collaboration with *Het Laatste Nieuws*, and re-re-shot (or re-re-hung) for my collaboration with the *Algemeen Nieuws*, in which Quick and Flupke has been appearing since September 1940. Being shot for the first time is the most terrible part; after that, I hear you get used to it.'

Hergé's cavalier reply at this stage shows just how aware he was of his position and how his actions would be perceived. He may have written the letter with a certain amount of jest, facetious in his response, but there was an underlying degree of fear within him as the events of the war unravelled and his future path became clearer.

In autumn 1943, while Hergé's fate was becoming apparent, he was still engrossed in his work, and spent a great deal of time and energy persuading Edgar Jacobs to collaborate with him on re-writing the early adventures of Tintin. Jacobs already felt swamped with work of his own, and it took a significant amount of insistence from Hergé before Jacobs acquiesced.

They eventually formed a contract with Hergé hiring Jacobs from 1 January 1944 as a collaborator, with the proviso that Jacobs would only work one morning each day while he was finishing his other work. Despite Jacobs acting as a collaborator on projects with Hergé now, the comic strip still only carried Hergé's signature, which he said was strictly for business reasons; this would later become a source of contention.

Jacobs set to work rewriting and colouring the early books. He started on *Tintin in the Congo* first, followed by *The Blue Lotus*, then *King Ottokar's Sceptre*. Hergé enjoyed having Jacobs work on projects with him and was impressed with his style, and it soon became clear that Jacobs was more than just a part-time worker. The pair were very close and would often go out drinking together, and they even once had a snowball fight. Hergé used Jacobs as a model from whom he drew various poses that characters adopted in the story, and he even sent him to research Incan material at the Cinquantenaire Museum. Hergé would discuss all his projects with Jacobs and as they became even closer, he asked him to help with his new Tintin story.

They had long discussions to prepare the scenarios for *The Seven Crystal Balls* and *Prisoners of the Sun*. The pair had a good energy together and would bat ideas back and forth quickly. Hergé had a great sense of humour, which meant that any discussion – even if it had moments of tension – relaxed immediately. He saw the funny side of a situation right away and couldn't help pointing it out, so he and Jacobs got on famously. They were on the same page and both were committed to producing a new and exciting adventure for Tintin.

Jacobs would later talk specifically about the parts he had added to the stories as he was not given a writer's credit, including the idea of the crystal balls and even the title of the book. In *Prisoners of the Sun*, he contributed the idea of the falling train, as well as the subterranean passages that provided access to the temple.

Hergé enjoyed working with Jacobs and although they were different in many ways, they complemented each other perfectly. Jacobs brought a great deal of cultural depth and richness, as well as graphic realism, and Hergé added a sense of plot through action and a clarity of line that is the hallmark of the Tintin series.

The results of this fortuitous collaboration speak for themselves. *The Seven Crystal Balls* shows a marked difference to *Red Rackham's Treasure* – details flood the scenes, which are vivid and meticulously researched. They inspired each other to push themselves to create arguably the greatest story in the series yet.

In this story, Tintin and Captain Haddock investigate the abduction of Professor Calculus and examine a mysterious illness which has affected the members of an archaeological expedition to Peru.

As with the previous two stories, *The Secret of the Unicorn* and *Red Rackham's Treasure*, *The Seven Crystal Balls* was designed as part of a double book, the second part of which was as yet unnamed, but would become *Prisoners of the Sun*. Hergé planned for the first story to set out the mystery, with the second story involving the characters going on a trip to uncover the answers.

The use of an ancient curse from an Egyptian mummy came from the stories of the curse of Pharaoh Tutankhamun's tomb, which Hergé had also used in *Cigars of the Pharaoh*. Hergé was keen to make all the details as realistic as possible and used the mummified Incan corpse from the Cinquantenaire Museum as inspiration for the mummy of Rascar Capac.

The background details were also drawn from real examples, such as the Opel Olympia 38 car in which Calculus's abductors escaped from the police.

The inspiration behind Professor Tarragon's house was an address on Avenue Delleur in Brussels, which Jacobs had found. The pair stood outside to meticulously sketch the building, and as soon as they had finished, two grey cars containing German soldiers pulled up and they realised that the house had been requisitioned by the Schutzstaffel (German SS). The pair had had a lucky escape; if they had been caught sketching the property, they would have been taken in for interrogation.

Hergé also included a number of characters from previous adventures, such as Professor Cantonneau from *The Shooting Star* and General Alcazar from *The Broken Ear*; Bianca Castafiore from *King Ottokar's Sceptre* also made an appearance.

While Hergé was greatly enjoying working with his friend and was producing some of his best creative work, the rest of his life was not in such great shape. The war was about to end and that brought anxiety and unrest for the Remis, who were aware how their actions during the Occupation would have been perceived. Hergé worried about what would happen after the war, and was chronically overworking himself.

In London, lists of 'inciviques' or 'non-civic-minded citizens' were being prepared, and even while the country was still under Occupation, there were more and more attacks on collaborationists in 1944. It was a tense time for many in the country.

Hergé contacted Charles Lesne at the end of April to say that he was unable to work as he had been unwell. For the past few weeks he had been ill with a list of ailments that included the flu, sinusitis and earache. He had been overworking himself to the point that he now felt deflated and incapable of working.

Soon his general malaise gave way to a more specific condition – Hergé started to talk of suffering from depression. Although he had probably suffered from this before, at this point in time the depressive episode was more severe, and led to Hergé's first breakdown. He was unable to work, and so *The Seven Crystal Balls* was brought to an abrupt halt in *Le Soir* on 6 May.

Hergé took time out to rest and recuperate, but he worried about the political situation, and feared retribution from those who accused him of being a collaborator. The fear was not unfounded – many accused of being collaborators had already been killed by the Belgian Resistance. Around the time of the Normandy landings by the Allied forces, Hergé would often use the phrase 'Lord, liberate us from our Protectors and protect us from our Liberators'.

After taking nearly two months off to rest, Hergé finally felt well enough to return to work. There was an announcement in *Le Soir* on 5 July declaring that Tintin and Snowy were returning:

> *'Perhaps, since you haven't heard anything about them lately, you have been afraid, dear readers, that something bad had happened to them? Nothing of the sort! Tintin and Snowy were simply waiting for our excellent associate and friend Hergé to return to better health, as he was sick for a few weeks. And, with Hergé now happily feeling much better, very soon we will again see the entertaining illustrations that show the newest adventures of Tintin in the columns of Le Soir.'*

The Seven Crystal Balls restarted in *Le Soir* on 7 July 1944, much to the relief of the readers, and included a summary of the story so far.

Meanwhile, the Liberation came closer. King Leopold III and the princes were transferred to a castle near Dresden in Germany. The people who had collaborated with the Nazis during the Occupation started to flee the area. Hergé and Germaine were unsure what to do and deeply anxious about the situation. They went to visit Abbot Wallez in Aulne during August 1944, as Hergé would often turn to him in times of uncertainty and struggle.

Regardless of the tense political situation and impending liberation, Hergé continued with the comic strip regularly until it was interrupted again on 2 September 1944. This would be the last instalment of the Tintin comic strip that *Le Soir* would publish.

The Allied forces liberated Brussels from German occupation on 3 September and the pirate edition of *Le Soir* immediately folded. Just a few days later the entire staff of the pirate *Le Soir* were sacked and new editorial staff were employed.

Chapter 8

Although the war was over, for Hergé, the battle had just begun. A leaflet had been produced by the Resistance fighters entitled the 'Gallery of Traitors', and he was listed twice as a collaborator, once as Georges Remi and once as Hergé, along with his picture and address.

The pamphlet declared his misdemeanours included offering his services to De Becker. It also stated under his picture – 'Writer for the wartime *Le Soir*. Impossible to get any information about this individual. All that we have learned is that he must be closely watched.'

The leaflet goes on to say that the crimes committed by the people they had listed were known and proven, and that they planned to punish these individuals pitilessly. Hergé feared he would be attacked after he learned of this call to arms, and the Remis lived in a state of panic.

On 3 September at midnight, there was a knock on his door. Hergé, not knowing what to expect, was met with a band of vigilantes asking for his arrest, but they left soon after without him. This was the first of four separate incidents in which Hergé would be arrested and then subsequently freed by the State Security, the Judiciary Police, the Belgian National Movement, and the Front for Independence.

Indeed, on 7 September, Hergé was interrogated and released. The next day, the Allied High Commission issued a statement declaring that any journalist or photojournalist who had helped produce a newspaper during the Occupation was for the time being barred from practising his profession.

Hergé was distraught – he was now blacklisted and unemployed. The day after, the Judiciary Police arrived on his doorstep to search his home. They found nothing incriminating but took him to the central Brussels police station where he was interrogated again. Here he spent a night in jail, together with around twelve other inciviques, such as Paul Herten. Herten had acted as editor of *Le Nouveau Journal* during the war, and he was punished for this – he was executed by firing squad soon after.

Hergé was released but three days later, the Belgian National Movement surrounded the house with sub-machine guns in hand. They interrogated Hergé, and he was again released. Two days later, the Front for Independence burst in and once again, Hergé was interrogated and subsequently let go.

A newspaper with links to the Belgian Resistance called *La Patrie* issued a satirical comic strip entitled *The Adventures of Tintin in the Land of the Nazis*, where Hergé was shown to be a collaborator.

After the latest arrest, Hergé was left alone for a while, nerves shattered and utterly exhausted. As there were over twelve similar groups and organisations keen to enact revenge on those they considered to be collaborators, Hergé feared they would keep coming one by one to arrest him, but he was left in peace – for the time being.

Hergé continued to work as usual, but isolated himself from the outside world as much as possible to shut out the troubles. Germaine was an enormous help to him at this time. She supported Hergé and kept a clear head, showing a huge amount of courage and nobility in the face of all the hostility they experienced.

After the war had ended, the people of Belgium needed to obtain a 'certificat de civisme' which was the official certificate of good citizenship, awarded by the bourgmestre or the police commissioner. Without the certificate, citizens weren't able to work or access services such as the tram system; they couldn't even ride a bike or own a dog. As he had worked for *Le Soir* under the Occupation, Hergé had little chance of obtaining this crucial document on his own, and without it, was not able to work for any of his former publications.

In any case, after the war ended, the real owners of the newspapers and other businesses returned to the city and took control of their companies. They were furious with the people who had used their publications during the war to make pirate editions and started to take action against those involved. Hergé was a *persona non grata*.

He wrote to Charles Lesne on 19 September in a more reflective state, looking back on his actions and decisions. He felt that regarding the war, he had been a pessimist. He said that everything had happened in the flash of an instant, and he was just grateful that although this was the second time his country had been invaded, it had been, on the whole, preserved miraculously. He said that two miracles in four years was a lot, and he hadn't dared to even hope for it. Implying that he thought the Nazis were going to be victorious, he suggested this was why he had decided to work under the Occupation.

Meanwhile, his old boss and mentor, Abbot Wallez, had been arrested for collaboration, as he had vocally supported the far-right Rexist Party during the war, and he was placed in Charleroi jail. Hergé was incredibly upset to hear this and was incensed that Wallez was being treated like a criminal. In Hergé's eyes, the abbot could do no wrong; he believed Wallez loved Belgium with all his heart and had only ever acted in the best interests of the country.

Many of Hergé's other friends and colleagues were also arrested and in a far worse predicament than him. Julien de Proft was arrested as a Nazi propagandist and he served at Saint-Gilles prison, before being released. Paul Werrie was being searched for, but so far had managed to evade his persecutors.

Marcel Dehaye spent fifteen days in prison at Namur before being released, while Hergé's friend and collaborator Paul Jamin and the rest of his family fled to Germany, as did Jose Streel and Gaston de Ruk, both of whom had been condemned to death in absentia.

Van Melkebeke and Robert Poulet were in prison at Saint-Gilles, along with Victor Meulenijzer, and Jean Libert was imprisoned at Forest, along with many others.

Hergé was distraught. His friends were in jail, and people hated him. He couldn't understand it. Towards the end of his life he said that this was the most painful time for him.

He thought all of his journalist friends were innocent and did not believe they had been working for the enemy during the war. Some of these people, who Hergé considered to be patriotic characters, were condemned to death for their actions during the Occupation and a few of them were even executed by firing squad. Hergé could not understand the vitriol that he and his cohorts faced, and felt it was a glimpse of absolute intolerance, and an awful, horrible time.

In 1973, however, he gave an interview where he described the situation differently. He said he realised just how naive he had been at that stage, and described how his experiences after the Second World War made him more wary. He said, 'The result of my naivete at the time was limited to stupidity – one might even say imbecility. I drew for the newspaper *Le Soir* during the war, which was controlled by the Germans, and I must admit that it should have dealt a death blow to my subsequent career. All of it was looked on poorly after the war, and rightly so; I had stayed on to work at a "guilty" newspaper. But I had to think about my survival, didn't I? And above all, I never did anything other than draw my comic strips during the war. I did no German propaganda. I wouldn't consider myself as what they called an "incivique".'

The former editor of the pirate *Le Soir*, Raymond De Becker, was in jail. He later wrote that many people who collaborated, and who lacked neither intelligence nor sincerity, found themselves awakening from this episode as if from a state of drunkenness. He described how they hardly remembered the real nature of their past actions and wondered how they could truly have acted as they incontrovertibly did.

While the people involved struggled with jail and the morality of their own involvement, Hergé withdrew into himself and fell into a deep depression that would dog him for the next fifteen years.

Despite his declining mental health, he managed to work on his books, but he was still banned from working for newspapers. He took this opportunity to finish colouring *Tintin in the Congo* and worked on *King Ottokar's Sceptre*. Edgar Jacobs was a particular support to him at this point, visiting daily, sometimes even offering to protect the couple in case anyone threatened them.

Charles Lesne was also very supportive, despite being on a different side during the war. He started to think about launching Hergé's books in Switzerland, Canada, Holland and Britain.

Hergé's agent, Bernard Thiery, was less helpful and while Hergé wanted to continue the relationship, he insisted he should also be able to act on his own behalf. The agent would not agree to this and said that the reason things weren't moving faster with regards to branded postcards and puzzles was because Hergé was implicated as a collaborator.

In total, there were more than 600,000 people thought to have collaborated under the Occupation, but the courts convicted just 40,000 for this crime. Hergé was not convicted but he was widely criticised, and things were about to get worse for him and his family.

During this period, all of Hergé and Germaine's family struggled with the stress of the events of the war and the ensuing liberation. In addition to this, in October 1944, Germaine's beloved father died. She was grief-stricken and remained in a melancholic state for months.

At the end of 1944, Hergé's mother, Elisabeth, was listening to the radio when there was an announcement of a Lieutenant Remi's death. After hearing this, she was sure her beloved younger son, Paul, had been killed and she suffered a violent nervous breakdown. Although they discovered quickly that her son was safe, Elisabeth did not recover from her dark state.

She suffered from delusions and at one point became convinced that her son Paul had been released from the German jail and returned to Belgium, but he was being hidden from her by his wife, Jeannot. Elisabeth hurried to their house and pounded on the door, with Jeannot and her daughter Denise huddled together, frightened of Elisabeth's violent outbursts.

While Germaine was grieving for her father and Hergé was struggling with the aftermath of the Purge, Elisabeth had another episode on 21 April 1945. She was well aware of Hergé's problems and this was a constant worry for her. Combined with the thought that her other son, Paul, had died, along with the stress the war had placed on everyone in the country, this all proved too much for Elisabeth, who was already predisposed to health issues.

She was taken to the Titeca psychiatric clinic where she was given electroshock therapy. The doctors were optimistic and she was transferred to the Institut Saint-Camille between Brussels and Louvain, and it was expected that she would make a full recovery.

Paul Remi returned home on 5 June, having spent the last five years trapped within the barbed wire fences of the German prisoner of war camp, from which he had often tried to escape. Paul and Hergé met the very next day. While Paul had fought for his country, Hergé had been working on a 'pirate' version of the biggest paper in Belgium and reaping the rewards. Now it was Hergé who was struggling with the aftermath of the war, while Paul was relieved to be returning home as a hero.

The reunion was difficult, but the brothers went to see their frail mother in the Institut Saint-Camille together. They hoped that having

Paul visit would help Elisabeth, but the trip did not go well. Although she recognised Paul, she started raving again immediately and the brothers realised they would have to wait and be patient, and simply hope for a full recovery for their very ill mother.

This period marks a definitive low for Hergé – his mother was chronically ill, his wife desperately grieving her father, his career and name in tatters and he was banned from working on newspapers.

However, in September 1945, Hergé was thrown a lifeline. The brother of the former director of *Le Vingtième Siècle*, Pierre Ugeux, contacted Hergé about a project he wanted him to help with. A friend of his, Raymond Leblanc, was keen to start a new children's weekly along the lines of *Le Petit Vingtième* but put together in a more modern style.

Leblanc had returned to Belgium as a war hero, and after the country had been liberated, he founded a publishing house called Yes. He was a shrewd businessman, and knew that he had to get authorisation to publish quickly as it was the only way to get paper. He was very aware that possessing paper was the key to success in 1944, and would even say that at that time anything could be printed and it would sell as people had such a great need for information. Publishing quickly became an extremely profitable occupation.

The team behind the new publication was not immediately convinced that another youth weekly would be a success as there were already a number of similar titles. But they had access to Hergé through Ugeux, and if the weekly were to be called *Tintin*, they felt it couldn't be anything other than a success. Leblanc had read *Le Petit Vingtième* as a child and was a huge fan of Hergé.

But first they needed to persuade the cartoonist. Hergé liked the idea, but was less than enthusiastic given his current situation. He was especially concerned by how the political authorities would receive the publication. Indeed, a couple of Leblanc's acquaintances had previously considered teaming up with Hergé on a similar project, but had abandoned the plan due to his poor reputation in the aftermath of the war.

However, although he was worried how people would react to the magazine, Hergé was not in a position to turn down offers, and an association with a celebrated war hero could only help his tattered reputation. Hergé also needed to acquire the 'certificate of civisme' and Leblanc had connections with people who could help smooth this process along.

Pierre's brother, William Ugeux, the former editor of *Le Vingtième Siècle* and an important figure in the Resistance movement, was now head of the National Information Bureau and answered directly to the prime minister. Leblanc pleaded Hergé's case to William, who knew Hergé well from his time at *Le Vingtième Siècle*. He thought Hergé had been more inept than traitorous and said that he was politically naive.

To err on the side of caution, he ordered Hergé's file to be examined before sanctioning the all-important 'certificate of civisme'. Hergé never saw the contents of his file, but he might have been consoled to hear the opinions within. Back in March 1945, Vincotte, the military auditor wrote to the auditor-general to say that he was inclined not to press charges against Hergé, as he felt it would make a mockery of justice to attack the author of inoffensive drawings for children.

However, he investigated the situation fully, despite his reservations. In the current climate, they were working under the assumption that they should prosecute anyone who worked with the collaborationist press, even if their personal contribution did not constitute propaganda.

Vincotte was aware that due to the popularity of Hergé's work, he was one of the people who did the most to cause *Le Soir* to be purchased during the Occupation. The military auditor knew he would have to prosecute others such as literary and sports reviewers, whose articles were not inflammatory in themselves, and he was aware that Hergé could be said to have done as much and maybe even more than they did to boost the sales of the newspaper.

He clearly did not find the material in *The Shooting Star*, which appeared during the Occupation in the 'pirate' *Le Soir*, to be examples of Hergé's collaboration and was keen to let him off any charges. Despite this, the auditor-general asked for an expert's report from the Central Documentation Bureau. In November 1945, Vincotte wrote to the auditor-general to say that the investigation opened on Hergé had not revealed any new evidence since 11 September 1944. He added that there was no evidence of propaganda-related comic strips, no memberships of pro-German groups, not even the hint of any feelings favourable to the former Occupying force.

Vincotte went even further with his proclamations on Hergé to say that at that time, the number of newspapers published was limited by the Germans and that every newspaper was sold due to the limited numbers and information available.

The profit made by the newspaper was not determined by the content or its success, it was determined by the allowance of paper it had been given by Germany. He went so far as to suggest a defence for Hergé and others in a similar position by saying that by working for *Le Soir* and taking up space in the newspaper with children's drawings or by talking about art, fashion or sports, they actually reduced the room available in the paper for German propaganda, and thereby acted patriotically.

Clearly, Vincotte and Ugeux's campaign to help Hergé was working, as at the end of December 1945, Hergé received the news that his criminal case had been dismissed. He still wasn't eligible for the 'certificate of civisme', but it was a step in the right direction and a huge relief for the Remis.

Hergé felt he could progress with the idea of the magazine dedicated to Tintin and would often meet with Leblanc to discuss the details. In March 1946 they signed a five-year contract, and so the *Tintin* magazine was born. Soon after, Hergé received his 'certificate de civisme', and it seemed as though the end of this ordeal was in sight and they were finally in a position to move forward.

However, the storm was not yet over. Hergé's mother was still very unwell. He would visit as often as he could, but she no longer recognised him. His mother died on 23 April 1946, aged sixty. Hergé was distraught, as was his father who doted on his beloved wife. It had been a terrible year for the Remis, and his father would not recover from this awful blow for a long time.

Hergé was always tight-lipped and stoical when it came to family, but the death of his mother was particularly painful to him. He felt he had never really known her or had real contact since he had been a young child, and he lamented their distant relationship. The grief and stress for him was overwhelming, but he could not take time to rest and recuperate as soon the trial would begin for the pirate version of *Le Soir* and those charged with collaborating.

Chapter 9

Although he wasn't directly involved in the trial, Hergé nevertheless felt very invested in the events and attended the court to support his friends who stood accused.

The trial began on Monday, 3 June 1946, for the 'pirate' version of *Le Soir*, and in a strange twist of fate, the magistrate happened to be Vallee Poussin, who had acted as editor-in-chief of *Le Vingtième Siècle* after Wallez had left, and someone that Hergé knew well.

Although Hergé was there as support only, his name was mentioned in the proceedings from day one, when the attorney of Julien De Proft, one of Hergé's friends, said he was surprised that the author of Tintin was not being prosecuted, even though he had contributed to the success of the 'pirate' *Le Soir*.

Just three days later, one of the writers of the real *Le Soir* newspaper also complained that Hergé was not being prosecuted, adding that he thought the people who collaborated by contributing 'space-filling' material should be brought to trial as they had been complicit.

Hergé had indeed had a lucky escape. While he had emerged relatively unscathed from the war, Marcel Dehaye, a good friend of his and the artistic editor on the 'pirate' *Le Soir*, was castigated for his involvement.

Dehaye had written the 'Jean de la Lune' letters, and when it was mentioned that these were entirely benign in nature during the court proceedings, the prosecutor said, 'They are entertaining, certainly, but they are like the silver wrapper on a poisoned bonbon.'

Hergé wondered why he wasn't held to the same standard, and while he felt guilty that he had escaped, he was also indignant that his friends were being punished so harshly. Indeed, some of Hergé's other close friends were in even more dire situations.

Paul Jamin, who Hergé had worked closely with on *Le Petit Vingtième*, was initially condemned to death for his drawings in *Le Pays Reel* and the *Brusseler Zeitung* during the Occupation. This was later reduced to life in prison. Jamin wrote to Hergé, who replied a month later.

In July 1946, Hergé wrote to tell his friend that he was convinced that it would all work out okay in the end. He reassured him that people were relaxing slowly but surely and he was sure they would eventually realise the punishment they had given to Jamin was not at all appropriate for the crime he had committed. He hoped that his friend would be released from prison one day soon and would emerge having matured and been shaped by the terrible trial.

Meanwhile, Germaine had left the city to take her mother on a visit to the coast, visiting the popular Rooster beach to escape the stress of the trial. Hergé stayed behind to work on the launch of *Tintin* magazine. While Germaine was away the verdicts from the trial were announced. Hergé wrote to tell her of the news, and was more direct than he had been with Jamin. He said that there had been leniency on one side with Meulepas, for whom they'd asked for seven years, and would serve just four. For De Proft they had asked for five years, but he was given just two; Brohee was also given two years and Colmant, for whom the prosecutors had asked for three years was given just one year to serve.

But he lamented the treatment of his other friends. De Becker was threatened with life in prison, but instead he had been condemned to death. Schaenen was given life in prison, despite the fact that the auditor had recommended a twenty-year sentence. Hergé called the judgments grotesque and ignoble, and found the whole situation torturous, especially as De Becker's mother had been in the courtroom as the judgments were given out. She had misunderstood what was said and thought that her son had received life in prison as predicted. She had congratulated Meulepas, who couldn't bear to tell her the truth.

Hergé struggled with the pressure of the trial and missed his wife dearly. The previous few months of turmoil had brought them even closer together. He wrote that he felt it was just recently he had been writing to her at the same place she was staying in, the Joli-Bois hotel, but then he had written to her as Miss Germaine Kieckens, and now she was his beloved wife. He cherished her greatly, and told her that she was still the same young girl he loved and that he cared for her even more than he had done in the early days.

Germaine was feeling the same. She wrote back to him the next day, saying how strange it was that they had been having the same memories. She couldn't believe that they had been together for fifteen years already.

The recent events had greatly affected Germaine. She was shaken up and felt so sensitive at that time that the smallest thing would make her cry. Although she and Hergé had a strong relationship and were getting on well, Germaine felt nervous. She said that their happiness seemed almost too perfect and it made her afraid, but she could not pinpoint exactly what she was fearful of. She even recently said to Hergé while his friend and collaborator Jacobs was present that she was sending him an SOS. She was weary and afraid, and these feelings would turn out to be incredibly prophetic, as their happiness would soon be tested.

Germaine had lost her father two years earlier and still grieved for him, and was incredibly upset at the events that had unfolded in Brussels. She put her feelings of worry down to this, and vowed to change her schedule when she returned to Brussels, deciding to work even more closely with Hergé.

While the trial was going on and Hergé's personal life was slowly crumbling, he still continued to work. He was in the middle of preparing *Tintin* magazine with Raymond Leblanc and Georges Lallemand and set about assembling a crack team of cartoonists.

First, Hergé recruited friend and artist-extraordinaire Edgar Jacobs. Next was Jacques Van Melkebeke, who became the editor-in-chief. The pair brought along a friend, Jacques Laudy, the son of a painter.

The final member of the team was Paul Cuvelier who, at just 22 years of age, was the youngest in the group and was introduced to Hergé by Paul Hennebert, the nephew of Abbot Wallez. He had had his first drawing published in *Le Petit Vingtième* when he was just 7 years old. When he came to the interview, Hergé was impressed with the young man and wrote a gushing letter to him a few weeks after the meeting, inviting him to come and work with them and to bring his drawings.

Hergé was ecstatic to meet him and felt he had found a new artist with an extraordinary talent. He urged Cuvelier to work hard and told him he had such true talent, that if he did work well, he would become a great artist. He encouraged Cuvelier to produce his own comic strip which would result in *Corentin*, inspired by the many stories he used to tell his younger brothers.

While Hergé was the artistic director of the new magazine, and all pages had to meet with his approval, Van Melkebeke was responsible for running the rest of the publication.

Leblanc had helped Hergé out enormously, but Hergé was still cautious of him, as it seemed that Leblanc was very much the businessman and concerned about sales above all else. Hergé felt that he was a very upright and honest fellow, but dangerously naive, and for that reason would remain slightly distant from him.

The group worked well as a team, but Hergé's reputation as a collaborator was still having an effect on business. It was hard to find a printer willing to work on the project as most did not want to be affiliated with him. However, they eventually found someone willing to work with them despite the negative connotations of Hergé's name, and the results were excellent.

Leblanc organised an aggressive launch for the magazine, with publicity films being shown in the cinemas of Brussels and flyers plastered on every shop and newspaper stand.

The first issue was released on 26 September 1946 all across Belgium, with an ambitious initial print run of 60,000 copies. It was an enormous success and they sold out within a few days. After just three days it was impossible to find a single copy of the first issue anywhere. They decided to increase the print run of subsequent issues to 80,000.

More than that, in the first issue they had asked for their readers' opinions of the magazine, and they were overcome by the avalanche of mail they received as a result. The loyalty of the fans caught them completely by surprise and it was a welcome they hadn't even dared to hope for.

For Hergé, this was a redeeming moment and a high point in an otherwise awful year. He had been reluctant to start the project, partly due to concerns over how he would be perceived, and partly due to all the hatred that had been directed at him and his former colleagues in the days after the war, during the Purge and also during the subsequent trial. He did not expect to be welcomed back so warmly and it was a much-needed tonic after the turmoil of recent events.

The first issue of *Tintin* proudly continued the adventure that had stopped so abruptly in the 'pirate' edition of *Le Soir*, which had been *Prisoners of the Sun*. To make the move as seamless as possible, Hergé had summarised the story so far using the clever technique of a press clipping, and so the adventure could resume.

As well as the main comic strip featuring Tintin, there were also many other sections starring the protagonist as well as other major characters, such as 'Tintin Speaks to You', 'Interviews with Captain Haddock', 'Tintin Tells a Story' and 'Comments by Major Wings'. The popularity grew and grew, and by December 1946, the paper added more pages with features such as 'Tintin Scouting', 'Tintin Sports' and a section that was purportedly written by Cuthbert Calculus.

The magazine proved to be a huge success, however, Hergé's detractors soon began to vocalise their dissent. In 1946, the journalists' union was an extremely powerful force to be reckoned with, and it sought to ostracise everyone who had published writing during the war.

Former *Le Soir* journalist Fernand Demany was fiercely opposed to the *Tintin* magazine, and he said it would bring back painful memories for those who remembered the 'pirate' edition of *Le Soir* to which Hergé had contributed.

Traditionally, Hergé had been given a great deal of support from the Catholic church, but in the days after the war, the tide had turned. In October 1946, the Catholic newspaper *La Cite Nouvelle* launched a scathing attack on the artist decrying his actions.

They were incensed that, as they saw it, the 'German-sympathising cartoonist' had not been prosecuted and he was now authorised to publish a *Tintin* magazine, and they were angry he had been given an official paper supply. They called him any number of names, such as a 'bad citizen', a 'traitor' and said he was someone who had served the enemy in return for a substantial salary. They were furious that he was now free to draw and contribute to a publication again and said he would be free to 'put his little brigade of 'Hitler Youth' back in business'. They poured vitriol on his character and his work, asking if the children of the people who had been killed by the Germans should accept someone who had worked to amuse kids for the benefit of the enemy, adding that there was a cell waiting for Hergé in Saint-Gilles prison.

Although the general population were more than happy to welcome Tintin back, some were still unable to forgive Hergé for his actions during the war. The furore around the magazine continued until Vincotte, the military auditor, felt obliged to step in again. Although the auditor-general felt there was no case for the prosecution of Hergé, the matter was still taken up in Parliament and a committee was formed to discuss the issue.

However, Hergé avoided any real repercussions, but his colleague, Van Melkebeke, on the other hand, was not so lucky. He had already served months of detention in 1945 and was banned from exhibiting any of his work for ten years, but worse was to come. In October 1946, when the attacks on *Tintin* magazine grew ever fiercer, he stood trial for his articles in *Le Nouveau* journal during the Occupation, in particular, one article on the trial of members of the Resistance.

He was sentenced to ten years in prison, but as he was not arrested straight away, he continued to work on *Tintin* magazine. Leblanc was unhappy with the situation and reluctant to allow Van Melkebeke to continue to work for him. When he heard the police were about to arrive at the Tintin offices from his friends on the National Security Bureau, he ordered that all traces of Van Melkebeke be stripped from the area. He named one of his friends, Andre Fernez, as editor-in-chief.

Van Melkebeke slipped away into the shadows. He continued to work and contributed to *Tintin* magazine while he remained in hiding from the police, with Hergé acting as a go-between. He worked on each of the comic strip adventures within the publication, although Leblanc had no idea this was going on.

Meanwhile, other issues were quietly fermenting under the surface. Jacobs was working part-time on the magazine, contributing the comic strip *The Secret of the Swordfish*, which was extremely popular, and Hergé loved his work. The pair made an excellent team and they both realised how well they worked together on the whole, although Jacobs was becoming unhappy with some aspects of their work.

In the contract they had together, Jacobs was promised 10 per cent of the author's fees for every project on which he worked – apart from *The Adventures of Tintin*, which he didn't feel was fair. He was also unhappy with the split of fees for other work. For the *Voir et Savoir* comic series, Hergé drew the characters and received 55 per cent of the royalties, while Jacobs, who drew all the backgrounds and accessories, which was a larger and more complex job, received just 45 per cent.

Jacobs was frustrated with Hergé's working practises and would later talk about how demanding Hergé could be. He would criticise miniscule details in Jacobs' work, such as a drawing of a plane, when Jacobs felt it was obvious that the document they had used to copy the object from was at fault, rather than his drawing.

Hergé would often say that Jacobs could be quite difficult to work with, and Jacobs felt that Hergé was incredibly fussy in his attention to detail. Overall, they produced brilliant work together and Hergé was well aware of this. Eventually, he asked Jacobs to work with him full-time, but Jacobs was reluctant, concerned he might become stuck in his shadow. After taking a few days to think about the proposal, Jacobs told Hergé that he would stay with him if both their signatures could appear on the books.

Hergé was taken aback at the idea and asked for time to think about it. The following week, he spoke to Jacobs and told him that the editors at Casterman wouldn't go for the idea, but Jacobs was convinced that it was Hergé who would not accept a joint credit on their work.

It was at this point in early 1947 that Jacobs decided to leave the magazine and work for himself again. The departure of Jacobs was a huge blow to Hergé. He had thoroughly enjoyed collaborating with the artist, and preferred this way of working to the long hours of solitary drawing he had been accustomed to before.

At this point, he knew he had to replace Jacobs, and it would require an entire team to cover all the jobs he had done. It was this departure that was the catalyst for Hergé to set up what would become Studios Hergé.

Jacobs had brought a great deal of talent to *The Adventures of Tintin*, adding a level of detail and sophistication that Hergé would find difficult to replicate. He left *Tintin* magazine to focus on his popular *Blake and Mortimer* series, and both men missed each other. Hergé was very disappointed that his friend and colleague had left, but the pair became close again soon after.

With Jacobs' departure, Hergé had a space to fill artistically but also within his personal life. At this point, many of his closest friends were languishing in jail, including De Becker, Poulet and Jamin. Hergé had even argued with Phillippe Gerard over the latter's conduct during the war and the two never saw each other again.

Marcel Dehaye, who had worked with Hergé on the 'pirate' version of *Le Soir*, now worked as Hergé's secretary, a post he had held since 1944, but he did not know a great deal about comics and did not fill the void left by Jacobs.

Hergé hired Guy Dessicy for some of the redesign and adaptation work. He was not as experienced as Jacobs, so Hergé decided to train him and even asked Van Melkebeke to give him a series of drawing lessons. Hergé would also explain his own methods of colouring which were very detailed and complex.

The complicated technique involved applying successive layers of watercolour which would allow foregrounds and backgrounds to be treated differently. The overall picture required six layers, with the most distant parts of the setting requiring just a single layer. Tintin's cheeks were done with a simple smudging stump and pastels. Dessicy learned quickly and Hergé was happy with the progress of his new team member.

Tintin magazine was developing well and Hergé began to recover slowly from the past few years of turmoil. However, it was at this point that Hergé's relationship with his agent, Bernard Thiery, which had always been difficult, finally fell apart.

Hergé found out that Thiery had been acting less than honestly. He had received a great deal more money than he had revealed to the cartoonist, and the agent had also hidden some elements of business from him. Hergé was furious at Thiery's underhanded manner.

In a long letter written on 8 May 1947, Hergé detailed the various issues he was concerned about and ended saying that given these conditions, it was no longer possible for him to trust Thiery and consequently he was breaking their contract. Hergé gave the man eight days to agree amicably, but after that deadline passed, he said he would take all measures the situation may necessitate.

Thiery wanted to meet with Hergé, but the cartoonist would not consider it. Thiery instead wrote a letter trying to explain the seemingly nefarious transgressions, but Hergé was not happy with his reply.

Hergé was struggling with stress, and the conflict only made this worse. He even ascribed the overwork and depression he experienced to the actions of Thiery and their hostile relationship. He was finding it hard to work and needed peace of mind and serenity to create the *Tintin* series.

Thiery disrupted this calm for Hergé and he was particularly disappointed as he felt that Thiery knew how important it was for him to have peace. In Thiery's initial pitch in 1942 he had assured Hergé that he would relieve him of any business worries in order to allow him to focus on his work in complete tranquillity, but in fact he had just created more business woes for the cartoonist.

Chapter 10

On 22 May 1947, Hergé turned forty. This milestone birthday is often a time of introspection, but for Hergé, he was at his lowest ebb. The aftermath of the war had taken its toll on the artist – he had friends in jail for their actions during the Occupation, and he struggled with feelings of guilt as he had not acted very differently to them. He was grieving for his mother, and his relationship with his brother was strained. The continuing conflict with his agent was draining him. Even his work, which he had done, head down, since leaving school, he found unfulfilling, and he was arguing constantly with Germaine, who had stuck with him and supported him in his work, and whom he had previously said he cherished so dearly.

His birthday was not a time for celebration. He was depressed, he wasn't sleeping and suffered terribly with outbreaks of boils and eczema as he often did in times of extreme stress or unhappiness. A bout of boils was one of the reasons he had been allowed to leave military service when the war had initially broken out. He was struggling again now with the same physical symptoms, as well as tiredness, which made him irritable.

Hergé saw a variety of doctors, and they all came to the same conclusion – he needed rest. Accepting their advice, he dropped his work midway through a Tintin story and, leaving Germaine behind in Brussels, he took Marcel Dehaye to stay with his friend Marius Chopplet who lived near the parish of Father Bonaventure Fieuillien. He asked Germaine to talk to Raymond Leblanc and explain the situation to him.

He needed rest and relaxation. His nerves were frayed and anything could upset him at this stage. It was when the kindly Father Fieuillien came to see him one day and asked for his opinion on some etchings he had done that Hergé realised quite how poor a state he was in.

After talking with the priest for a while, he excused himself and asked to leave. Marcel Dehaye accompanied Hergé and looked after him as he left to stretch out in the grass a distance away from the village. He was truly exhausted.

It was then he understood the condition he was in. Even the slightest thing, which in this particular case had been giving his opinion on the priest's etchings, left him completely drained and on the verge of tears. He wrote to Germaine to explain what had happened and how he was feeling.

Germaine was patient with her husband and replied soon after to reassure him that the conflict with his agent was being dealt with. To comfort her husband, she told him that the lawyers were dealing with the issue and that they were telling the agent he would lose the case. She consoled him and told him that everything would work out in the end, and added that the bad guys will be punished, 'just like they are in *The Adventures of Tintin*'.

Meanwhile, Hergé's colleagues at *Tintin* magazine were frantically trying to carry on, but without the star cartoonist, it was no easy task. The latest Tintin adventure, *Prisoners of the Sun*, had to stop, and on 19 June, the magazine made an announcement:

> '*Our friend Hergé needs a rest. Don't worry, he's doing fine. But in refusing to save his strength, in order to bring Prisoners of the Sun to you each week, our friend has overworked himself a bit. He will soon come back to us, thank goodness, and is even now preparing the next fantastic adventures of Tintin and his courageous companions. We will take advantage of this short intermission to publish, as many of you have requested, some new adventures of Quick and Flupke. We are confident that this will please you!*'

While the magazine floundered and tried to make do in his absence, Hergé was undertaking a much quieter journey, looking inward and analysing his life and his choices so far. He and Germaine exchanged many letters. They found this was a better way of communicating for them, as Hergé would open up more.

He thought about the mistakes he had made over the past few years. He wrote to Germaine, saying that he felt he had made the same number of blunders and errors that any normal man would make, possibly a few more, but that in the end it didn't matter, and that none of it really meant anything, as he had been happy.

But he wondered about his relationship with his wife, too, and asked Germaine if he had been as good to her as she had to him. He was going through a stage of deep introspection and when questioning himself on his relationships, found the answers he came to weren't always to his liking.

He realised that he had prioritised his work above all else, and that he had effectively neglected and abandoned his wife and chosen to please the public with his work instead.

This crisis he was struggling through made him realise he hadn't given enough time to his wife over the years, and that his work had taken over to such a degree that he vowed to make changes to his lifestyle. He promised they would have a second honeymoon, travel and relax together, and he wanted their life to be as happy and peaceful as possible.

However, his illness remained and he would continue to have fits of crying. Germaine was worried. She wanted her husband to slow down and to enjoy things more. Financially, he no longer needed to work all hours. With the author's fees from book sales alone, he was making a considerable sum. On 4 June she wrote to Hergé reminding him of this. She even said that they didn't need more money, adding that a lot of money usually meant a lot of problems. She reassured him of his legacy, too, telling him that he had a secure place in history and that people would speak of him in the future.

Hergé was well aware of his position. He felt he had been given love, happiness and fame easily, and knew he had a good life. But money no longer interested him. While he strove for financial security when he was younger, now he had achieved that he was no longer particularly interested, and treated it as a kind of sport.

He had been sent a particularly positive balance sheet from his publisher at Casterman, but it had just left him cold, and he felt disappointed in himself that he wasn't jumping for joy, as he had expected to be.

Hergé had always assumed that very rich people were simply blasé about their lifestyle, and now that he had achieved that level of wealth, he realised it was true. He was also disenfranchised with the idea of fame. It represented so little to him, and he would say to Germaine that, in the end, the game wasn't worth the price of admission.

He felt he was wearing himself out trying to be entertaining when it did not come naturally to him, and all for the pleasure of hearing the same accolades – something that no longer brought him happiness. He had an epiphany, realising that he had been exhausting himself for other people, when he had the extraordinary luck to have his wife to cherish, and he felt a fool. Having just turned forty, he was keen to make their relationship a happy one and desperate to make memories with his wife.

While Germaine was thrilled to receive such long, loving letters from her husband, who had generally been quite distant, she was concerned at the sudden change of heart about his work. Saying what an incontestable talent he had, she urged him to remember that he taught the little ones and entertained them at the same time, showing them what is just and good. To reassure him, she explained how much she appreciated how he did all this without any compromise and all by himself. She wanted him to know what a great job he was doing and that he should consider himself lucky to be so successful. Although it was sweet of him to want to dedicate his time to loving her, she worried he would tire of it quickly.

Germaine clearly felt a great deal of pressure at the time. Hergé was in crisis, and his sudden desire to stop working on the main project he had been creating for eighteen years and start devoting his time almost exclusively to her, would be an enormous change to their day-to-day life. Combined with Hergé's ill-health and his state of crisis, it perhaps shows that he was in search of something, or someone, who could finally make him happy, where everything else had failed.

Hergé replied to Germaine's concerns two days later, telling her that he was tired and worn out from all the praise. He was exhausted from drawing the same gag for the tenth time, tired of the sure laugh, tired of giving the best of himself, his essence, his life, in his work and tired of being a mechanism churning out stories from which he felt more and more detached.

His work was slowly but surely ceasing to interest him because it no longer fulfilled a need, whereas in the early days there had been a perfect harmony between him and his stories. He felt his true nature which he defined as honest and generous Boy Scoutism, hungry for heroism, thirsty for justice, defender of widows, orphans, and noble savages oppressed by the evil white men, was expressed spontaneously through Tintin. All of the work then had been fresh, young, spontaneous, neat and tidy – and yet he felt it was a vacuous nothing.

After working with many talented collaborators, Hergé could no longer work in the same way he had in the beginning; he now had to carefully plot and plan his storylines, and the colouring process was time-consuming. After working with Jacobs, there was an expectation for magnificent backgrounds and detailed scenes, which Hergé wasn't that interested in. For him, movement was key, and it seems that these additions, although a large part of why the Tintin series had done so well, were also part of the reason why Hergé fell out of love with the comic strip medium. He had lost his inspiration.

He no longer drew as easily as breathing, which had been the case not that long ago. He realised he was no longer 'Tintin', and felt he must make an enormous effort to find his former self again, to put himself back into the right frame of mind, so he could continue to draw and create.

Previously he had seen Tintin as an idealised version of himself – the hero he wanted to be, but he no longer thought of himself in that way, and no longer wanted to be the Boy Scout hero. His experiences during the war played a part in this disillusionment, for he realised he had not been the war-time hero that his brother had been, or that Tintin certainly would have been. While Hergé would flee or become ill at the hint of danger, there was a part of him that wanted to be a hero, braving danger and fighting the enemy for the good of the people.

Hergé had been greatly affected by the war, or specifically the Liberation and the subsequent Purge. He felt he had suffered so much from it, and his Boy Scoutism had been terribly damaged, and his view of the world turned upside down.

However, little by little, he was recovering and he felt that he was returning to his former self, but as a slightly different version. He had discovered that his character Tintin was no longer him, and that although he continued to live it was through a sort of artificial respiration that he must keep up constantly, and which he found completely exhausting.

Hergé was undergoing a metamorphosis of sorts. He had reached forty and was no longer the Boy Scout of the past. He mourned his loss of creativity when it came to Tintin, and as he made this realisation, he believed that the worst of his crisis would be over now that he understood what was troubling him.

He returned to Brussels briefly to sort out business matters, and wrote to Charles Lesne on 18 June for the first time since the crisis started, telling him that he had not been able to work for nearly a month due to his nervous depression, and he wasn't sure when he would be fit to work again. Indeed, Hergé had no intention of going back to work for quite a while yet.

A friend had suggested he should take Germaine on a break to Switzerland, recommending a road trip around the stunning countryside to enjoy some relaxing time together away from it all, and Hergé was set on the idea. After he returned to Brussels, he left again just as suddenly to take the trip he had wanted to go on for a long time. Both he and Germaine were very excited about the holiday, and on 22 June 1947 they left, crossing Luxembourg and France, until they reached Switzerland, where they travelled to Basel, Neuchatel, and Lausanne.

They planned to visit Geneva to sort out some of Hergé's business matters, but they were waylaid when they happened upon a little bolthole on the shores of Lake Geneva that would become a firm favourite for Hergé. It was the Hotel de la Plage in Gland, which he would say was 'the loveliest little chalet in all of Switzerland'. Hergé was truly happy for the first time in a long time.

The country was unscathed by war and they were not subject to food rationing as Belgium was at the time, and Hergé loved sampling the simple, abundant and varied food, especially the cheese and wine. He also loved the Helvetic cleanliness, and he and Germaine felt very at home in their room which had a view of the lake. He wrote to his friend and secretary, Marcel Dehaye, on 27 June to tell him how much he was enjoying himself.

For Hergé, it was the perfect trip – the sun was shining, the birds were singing, the lake gleamed, and he enjoyed wandering around the area in shorts. He loved Switzerland and thought that everything there was arranged around making life easier and happier for people. He found the Swiss to be very kind, and loved their gentle and musical accents. He said, 'The men are strong and tanned, the girls are pretty, and the children are charming.' There was nothing he did not like about the country.

Hergé and Germaine would while away the days swimming and rowing on the lake, walking in the mountains and enjoying the copious good food. It was another idyllic honeymoon for the jaded couple.

Managing to tear himself away briefly, Hergé took a trip to Geneva to deal with his business affairs. He had a meeting with the editors of *L'Écho Illustré*, where he discovered that his agent, with whom he was still trying to cancel his contract, had behaved poorly here as well. But this was a minor blip on an otherwise perfect break.

He would tell Germaine a hundred times a day how beautiful everything was and how happy he felt. The couple stayed in Switzerland and enjoyed an idyllic break before returning to Brussels on 10 July. Hergé wanted to stay away longer, but the pressure to return was mounting, particularly from Raymond Leblanc, who was keen for Hergé to carry on with the *Prisoners of the Sun* story in *Tintin* magazine, as more and more readers were beginning to complain about Tintin's absence.

On 14 August, Tintin returned to the magazine, with the cover announcing 'Finally, Tintin is back'. Leblanc was relieved and the readers were thrilled, but Hergé was not faring so well. He couldn't sleep again and worried chronically. Very soon it was clear that Hergé was suffering from exhaustion. He gave Leblanc a little notice this time, and on 25 September, he and Germaine travelled to Switzerland once again to give Hergé the rest he so desperately needed.

They stayed in the hotel in Gland they had fallen in love with, before moving on to the Pensione Rivabella in Brissago, Ticino, an Italian-speaking part of Switzerland, which was nestled along Lake Maggiore. Hergé loved the area and wrote glowing letters to Marcel Dehaye to tell him how happy he was. He also asked when the next Tintin instalment was due, although he was very reluctant to start work again.

For Hergé, who had always been so hardworking and diligent, work was now an inconvenience. He enjoyed long days with his wife – he and Germaine would go dancing and loved spending time with various Italians they met on holiday.

Hergé loved the Italian spirit, and felt their whole way of life revolved around love. He even commented that Mussolini had tried to change all that, ordering the people to 'believe, obey, fight' but that hadn't worked out for him as it went against the Italian ethos.

Germaine was enjoying this time with her husband – it was a rare and special adventure; one they hadn't experienced before. Carefree spontaneity had never been a mainstay of their relationship previously as work had always come first. Now for the pair it was all about love, travel and adventure.

They bought a map of Italy, and talked about how close Milan was to where they were, and noticed that Venice was not at the end of the world. Before she knew it, they were leaving Switzerland and heading off to Italy.

Despite Hergé's previous protestations that being wealthy did not matter to him at all, he was clearly enjoying the freedom this relatively new-found financial security afforded them, and with the war now over, they were free to travel. This period is one characterised by a newly rekindled adventurous side to Hergé – one that mixed the need for travel and excitement of the Boy Scout era with a rekindled romance with his wife, who had taken a backseat for many years.

They drove through Milan, Verona, and on to Padua until they eventually arrived in Venice. It was one of the happiest times they had ever had together, but it was not to last. They returned to Brissago, and then back to Brussels on 25 October, and Hergé reluctantly went back to work at *Tintin* magazine.

The summer of love for Hergé was well and truly over. Returning to work meant returning to a barrage of problems. Jacques Van Melkebeke was still in hiding and working for Hergé in secret, but the police eventually found him and he was sent to jail in December 1947, and would remain there for nearly two years.

This was a big blow for Hergé, personally and professionally, as he missed his friend, but he had also begun to rely on him for help with his work. He struggled to finish *Prisoners of the Sun* and tried to find another collaborator who could help him.

He asked Bernard Heuvelmans to come and work with him as he felt so washed out and completely drained of ideas. Heuvelmans had also worked for the 'pirate' *Le Soir*, and had assisted Van Melkebeke with Tintin material, so he knew all *The Adventures of Tintin* inside out. Hergé loved his wild imagination and was keen for him to help.

Heuvelmans accepted with enthusiasm and eagerly took up the thread of the story which Hergé had left at around halfway through. He invented incidents including the near-drowning of Snowy, the passage beneath the waterfall, and the rescue of the heroes, based on a newspaper clipping he had read about a solar eclipse.

Hergé was thrilled to have someone with so much talent to help him finish the story that had dogged him since he began *The Seven Crystal Balls* in the 'pirate' *Le Soir* in 1943, and the final instalment of *Prisoners of the Sun* featured in *Tintin* magazine in March 1948.

Around this time, Hergé toyed with the idea of making Tintin into a film. He often described his comic strips in cinematic terms and had for a long time wanted to make a Tintin film, but up until that point he had not had the necessary techniques or the money to fund the project.

After the war, however, two Belgian filmmakers wanted to make *The Crab with the Golden Claws* using puppets. The film had encountered financial issues, but they somehow managed to finish the work and it premiered on 21 December 1947. However, soon after, the filmmakers declared bankruptcy and fled to Argentina, much to the disappointment and frustration of Hergé.

It had been another stressful and difficult project for him during an already difficult period, but as time passed, he had become more interested in the medium of film again, and was keen to see his creations realised on the big screen in a more satisfying, and hopefully more successful, way.

On 9 April 1948, Hergé wrote to Walt Disney, describing how well his comic strips were doing in Belgium and elsewhere. He told Disney that he was arranging for his publisher to send him some of his books, so that he could judge for himself what the advantages of filming them might be.

Hergé was complimentary of Walt Disney's work, and told him he loved the way that his characters evolved. He realised his own work was quite different, with the adventures taking place in a realistic setting, but felt that it was the differences that would make a Walt Disney version of *The Adventures of Tintin* work well.

He was completely willing to defer to Disney in how things should be done and happy to place the matter entirely in Disney's hands. The willingness to give someone else complete control over his work is a world away from the earlier days, when Hergé wanted complete autonomy, which perhaps shows how keen he was to work with Disney, and perhaps also signifies that he wasn't so invested in Tintin as he once was.

Unfortunately, the project wasn't to be as Disney was just beginning work on *Cinderella* and had no time for other projects. The publicity director for Disney, Gil Souto, responded a couple of months later turning down the offer and even returning the series of Tintin books.

Hergé was disappointed, but told his friends that he hadn't expected anything else, and he appreciated the civil way in which the Disney company had told him that they weren't interested in the project.

Chapter 11

After all the recent disappointments, Hergé felt very disenfranchised and wanted to make some changes. He had spent much of 1947 escaping to Switzerland with Germaine, but by 1948 he wanted to make a more dramatic move.

A significant number of people who had been caught on the wrong side of the war in Belgium had moved to France or Switzerland after the war, but Hergé was thinking further afield – in South America.

In January 1948, he wrote to the Brazilian and Argentinian consuls asking for details on how to settle in their countries, and also made enquiries with various people about the publishing opportunities in those areas.

Argentina and Brazil had developed a reputation for being the countries of choice for Nazis and people accused of collaborating during the war. A move to these countries was a highly controversial plan at the time.

Hergé sent a letter on 8 April 1948 to his publisher Louis Casterman asking for help with his plans to move to South America. He was putting together all the documents he needed for the move, which included a certificate confirming Hergé's profession and a letter of recommendation.

He asked Casterman to define his profession as a 'Humorous cartoonist, author of numerous picture stories for children'. Hergé also requested a letter of recommendation or guarantee, which he left to the discretion of the publisher.

Despite the suddenness of the move, and the urgency with which Hergé was progressing, he was keen to reassure his publisher. He told him that it went without saying that he would not leave until the majority of the work in which Casterman had an interest in was finished, particularly *The Seven Crystal Balls* and *Prisoners of the Sun*. Hergé added he was sure he would still be able to provide them with the drawings necessary for the books once he had settled in his new country.

He didn't mention the move to the owner of *Tintin* magazine, Raymond Leblanc, or even his close friends, such as Marcel Dehaye. But he did divulge to Casterman that he would possibly not renew the contract with *Tintin* magazine, which would allow him time to complete other projects, such as finishing adding colour to the last book for the publisher.

Hergé had heard news of Pierre Daye, a former Belgian journalist and Nazi collaborator who had fled to Argentina after he was sentenced to death in 1946 for his work during the Occupation.

He wrote to him saying how thrilled he was to know that Daye was in good health and on top form. He was also happy to hear that, despite all the changes and tribulations, he hadn't forgotten Hergé and his cohorts, finding his kindness rare and heart-warming. He assured him there was barely a day that went past when they didn't mention all their friends scattered far and wide in the aftermath of the war.

Hergé also told him he was thinking of following in his footsteps, keen to leave their 'sad country' and settle permanently in Argentina, with no thought of ever returning. He quizzed Daye for information on newspapers in the country, and also asked if he could talk to the Department of Education and suggest that Hergé be allowed to launch a weekly magazine for children. He urged Haye to arrange visas 'in record time' for Hergé, Germaine, her mother, and their cat, Thaïke, to move out. He also requested visas for two others – a woman wishing to escape her abusive marriage and her daughter. Hergé mooted the idea of employing both women if he could find work in Argentina.

He was very excited about the trip, and told his friend he had just read a lovely story all about a sea voyage, which made him want to board the next cargo ship to Argentina. Hergé was desperate to leave the 'poor old broken-down Europe' for good and start a new life in the warm, promised land of Argentina.

But the plan wasn't to be. It is not certain why they didn't go ahead with the move, as Hergé was obviously very keen to leave as soon as possible. Perhaps Daye did not reply, but the most likely reason is that there was simply not enough work available for the cartoonist in Argentina, where there were already a great many American offerings, and the salaries were not as good as in Europe. Whatever the reason, Hergé was left deflated and stuck in 'poor, broken Europe' for the foreseeable future.

As fleeing the country to settle in Argentina was no longer an option, Hergé threw himself into other misguided adventures instead. While in

April he had set his mind on emigrating, he had to come to terms with the fact that it was not going to be possible, so the very next month in May, he bought himself a brand new Lancia and decided to go on another holiday to take his mind off the matters at hand.

Hergé wanted to take Germaine on a trip to his favourite place – Switzerland. However, this time he asked another woman to join them. This was Rosane, the daughter he had mentioned in the letter to Haye who had wanted to accompany Hergé and Germaine to Argentina, along with her mother. Hergé had known the family and Rosane for a long time. When she was just a child, he would take her to the cinema on Sunday afternoons with Germaine.

The odd trio set off for Switzerland in Hergé's new car and stayed in Brissago for a short while, before continuing on to Florence and then Rome. While in Brissago, Hergé embarked upon an affair with Rosane.

He later explained himself to his wife by saying that he had become unexpectedly caught up in the situation. He said he hadn't been careful – of Rosane or of himself. He had thought he could be a kind of uncle figure to her, and wanted to be someone she could come to for friendship and understanding, but this closeness had developed into something more. Their trip to Brissago had made their feelings all the more intense and they were swept up in the romantic atmosphere.

This was apparently not the first time he had been unfaithful, but it was the first time he had truly fallen in love with another woman. The three were in a bizarre love triangle while in the confines of a long road trip around Europe. The tension was unbearable. Hergé felt guilty and the worse he felt, the more he would take it out on Germaine, and he became nasty, dry and pitiless.

The group arrived back in Brussels on 12 June. Hergé was in turmoil and sought advice from Marcel and his father. He would also arrange meetings with Rosane and write long letters to her, all the while informing Germaine of what was happening in a rather misguided attempt to be open and fair. Hearing all the details of his affair hurt Germaine immeasurably.

It took Hergé a week to decide that he loved Germaine and could not lose her. He wanted to go on a trip to get away and try to piece their relationship back together after his devastating behaviour over the previous few weeks. They returned to Switzerland once again, and back to the Hotel de la Plage where they had been so happy the year before.

Almost as soon as they arrived, Hergé was preoccupied and melancholic. Germaine had become close to Marcel Dehaye, and wrote to him on 25 June describing the trip with Hergé. She told him they were living side by side like two very polite strangers, trying to carefully avoid the slippery areas. Germaine felt that Hergé didn't know what was happening to him, and she found it impossible to talk to her husband about anything. He would always give the same response to her – that he didn't know and that things just had to be that way.

She was frustrated and infuriated with him. Above all she wanted to know why he didn't just go and do what he wanted to do, why he didn't just live his life. Hergé was in turmoil and ultimately didn't know what he wanted from his life at that stage.

During the latest trip to Switzerland, Germaine began to regard Hergé as a seriously ill person, and the day after writing to Marcel, Germaine took a flight back to Brussels. She arrived at the airport where Marcel was waiting for her.

The next day, Marcel wrote to Hergé to tell him that he thought the temporary separation was a good thing for both of them, and that he should resist the temptation to return. Although the pair were struggling to live either together or apart, Marcel counselled that the best option at that point was to give each other space. He advised that as they had already hurt each other very much and said cruel, if not irreparable, things to one another, staying apart for a time was necessary.

Dehaye thought Hergé was being too introspective. He told him he was living with an obsession, and he should not ignore his fear. He suggested Hergé should make sure he exercised and should also focus on his work to take his mind off things.

Hergé agreed with at least some of what his friend had said. He wrote to Germaine on 28 June to tell her that he had been in the middle of an attack, which he thought was passing for the moment. He felt that the crisis had been a violent one, but it did not mean, as Germaine had thought, that he wanted something else. Hergé thought his crisis arose from realising the consequences of what had happened with Rosane, and he began to struggle. He told his wife he was not made for adultery; all he wanted was fidelity and that fundamentally, he was a faithful person.

Germaine allowed herself to let go of the relationship. She told her husband that he needed to do whatever he wanted to do, essentially saying that if he wanted to leave, he should leave.

But Hergé was adamant that he never wanted to leave her. He had thought about it, but when he did, he had immediately seen it would be a catastrophe. He met up with Rosane again when he was back in Brussels, but straight away told Germaine that he had seen her, and used this as an example of how he wanted to be honest and upfront with his wife. Hergé said that he instinctively wanted to stop himself from slipping into lies and betrayal, secret meetings and letters held for him at the post office. He admitted he had 'done wrong' in the past, but questioned if he had acted wrongly.

Hergé stayed at the Hotel de la Plage along Lake Geneva and tried to relax by swimming, reading and writing. Meanwhile, Marcel would write with details of his business affairs. They were moving Hergé's studio into the first floor of his house on Avenue Delleur.

In terms of work, Hergé was feeling less than enthused. In a letter to Germaine from 1 July, he told her that he felt he should write to Leblanc, but he didn't feel courageous or inspired enough. Germaine wanted him to explain the situation to the owner of *Tintin* magazine, but Hergé was reluctant, as he didn't know what he could say.

He didn't feel up to promising great things when he returned, as he felt tired and jaded with his work. The job in its current form hadn't been able to excite him or draw him back into the familiar routine. Germaine had been telling Hergé he should try to see clearly, and now that he could, he realised it would be simply impossible for him to put his whole life into his work again.

Hergé felt that unless he gave himself to the work entirely, it would just be a joyless chore. He was not worried about the reaction of the public if he was working without being fully invested; he said he knew enough techniques and bells and whistles to create something people would still enjoy, but he did not feel he could work in that way.

Nevertheless, despite his apathy and reluctance to work, Hergé had a binding contract with Raymond Leblanc that lasted until March 1951, so he knew he would have to return at some point in the near future.

Hergé wrote again to Marcel Dehaye a couple of days later to explain how he had fallen out of love with his work. He felt he had matured and the events of the last few years such as the Liberation and the subsequent Purge, the Thiery affair, and simply his age had taken its toll on him and he no longer felt able to continue with the comic strip. He found it difficult to return to work unless he could give everything to it, living purely for the work, comparing himself to Balzac, who he had recently been reading. He now wanted to paint, and felt that this was his future.

He remained in Switzerland and continued the tortured introspection, as well as reading, swimming, rowing and walking – all activities that reminded him of his happy Scouting days as a child. He also made friends with several of the locals in the area.

King Leopold III was in exile in nearby Pregny at the time with his family, while he waited to return to Belgium. The King invited Hergé to lunch, which he readily accepted. The two enjoyed a long afternoon together and even went fishing. He enjoyed his time with the exiled king, and they became friends, but Hergé knew that he would soon have to travel back to Brussels and return to work.

On 5 July 1948, Hergé wrote to Germaine to complain of his lack of inspiration. He asked her how he could try to love his work again when it had lost all interest for him, and wondered what he could do to make it have meaning again. He felt lost at this time and couldn't see a way forward.

He felt that if he had a subject he was passionate about, it might make all the difference. But the ideas he currently had at hand, the outlines of *Land of Black Gold* and *Destination Moon*, just left him cold. He didn't think those stories needed to be told, because he felt there was no necessity for them and he even went so far as to say that he couldn't care less about those subjects.

Meanwhile, Marcel Dehaye patiently organised Hergé's affairs in Brussels, but was beginning to get frustrated with his friend and boss. He had finished the studio move and was encouraging Hergé to paint, but also reminded him of the need to fulfil his obligations regarding the magazine and Leblanc. He told him that by signing the contract with the magazine, he had taken on serious commitments. At the beginning, the whole business had depended on him – on his talent and also his prestige. Dehaye reminded Hergé that the magazine was still not stable enough to do without him. He spoke frankly to underline the gravity of the situation in Brussels in terms of the business of the magazine. He said that capital had been invested and a considerable staff was earning a living from the publication. The whole organisation relied on Hergé to survive this episode undamaged. They needed him back and he needed to have courage and to behave responsibly.

Marcel went as far as to predict that when Hergé was no longer obliged to deliver any new drawings, he would stop doing anything at all. Dehaye thought that Hergé's current obsession with painting was really just an excuse he was giving himself to abandon his real work.

He was being scrupulously honest with his friend, and risking his wrath, in order to get everything out in the open. He asked what drawings Hergé had done for his own personal pleasure in the months of freedom and holiday that he had given himself recently. He also questioned what painting he had tried – where were the sketchbooks filled with drawings of Italy and Switzerland? Dehaye asked why he hadn't satisfied this need to draw and paint in the weeks that had just gone by.

But Hergé was defiant. He wrote back to say that he knew he was worth more than the work he had been doing. One day he was determined to do the sort of work that he felt he was worth, but he conceded that his friend was right – he couldn't simply abandon everything, he knew he had duties he would have to fulfil at some point soon.

As Hergé swam and read and made plans to return, Germaine was preoccupied with other matters. The person she admired most in the world, Abbot Norbert Wallez, had become very ill while in prison and was in a bad way. She hurried to see her dear friend.

Hergé was furious when he heard the news, and blamed the Purge for the Abbot's condition. He wrote to Germaine on 8 July to rant about the situation. He couldn't believe that the Abbot was ill, and called the people who had persecuted him 'monsters', blaming them for Wallez's illness. But this all brought out feelings in Hergé that he had not addressed before.

A little time later, he wrote again to Germaine about something that he had previously found difficult to talk about. He was deeply envious of Abbot Wallez and had found it incredibly difficult to live in his shadow.

Hergé knew how important he was to Germaine and all the things he represented for her. He knew that if Wallez were to disappear, it would be the loss of her last support, and he realised that Wallez's strength, calmness and kindness – his all-encompassing care for her – reassured and soothed his wife. He knew that she also found him to be a refuge, a support and a comfort.

This was particularly painful for Hergé as he also sensed that all of the things that Wallez offered Germaine, such as support, comfort and strength, were things that he simply wasn't able to give her. He ascribed this deficit to his age. He felt he was too young for his wife. She had been more mature than him from the beginning, and he still felt too immature. Even though he had tried, he just couldn't catch up.

He said he wanted to catch up with her in terms of maturity, but he felt he needed to grow very swiftly, by ten years in a single year, before he would be able to give her the feeling of security that she needed from him, but which he was sure that she had never felt, and would never feel.

Hergé added that he always felt as though he was still the young friend of their first meeting and that he had learned to be a man with her, clumsily, he conceded. While he was just beginning to develop, he knew she had already finished learning. He admitted he was jealous of Wallez, although he also loved him, but he couldn't escape the feeling that he had always been Germaine's second choice.

He now knew that Wallez had loved Germaine and that she loved him too with a very beautiful, pure and noble love. It was only now that he really understood their relationship.

Hergé wanted to start again with Germaine, and told her that nothing between them had been broken or lost, and absolutely nothing had been damaged. He even went as far as to say the opposite was true, that they had been brought closer together.

Hergé wrote this on 17 July and returned to Brussels on 23 July. However, far from being the harmonious reconciliation he had implied he wanted, it transpired that towards the end of his visit to Switzerland he had embarked upon another affair. The woman in question was a cousin of Jacques Laudy, one of Hergé's colleagues on *Tintin* magazine, and she was around thirty years old.

Germaine was devastated. He had told her that he loved another woman – he was completely, totally and madly in love. She wondered where that left her. It was a horrible, awful time for Germaine. She was suffering and in so much pain, she said she felt she could die.

She realised that her husband was also suffering – but for another woman. It was another betrayal and she mourned their relationship.

Hergé went on a trip to Ardenne with his friend Edouard Cnaepelinckx to think about the situation. His friend suggested leaving Germaine, but other friends implored him to stay with her. Hergé was at a loss as to which direction to take. He wanted time to heal, hoping there would be an event or a sign that would take him by the hand and show him clearly which path to follow.

He felt there were contradictory forces within him, more powerful than he ever imagined, that were taking over. Hergé had suddenly unshackled himself from his drawing board and had a thirst for living and living intensely. He told his friend Marcel he wanted to 'discover the world, people, bodies, everything,' and he was afraid to let any opportunities pass him by, he was afraid to let time slip away.

He needed a change, a renewal, and although he said he knew it was his 'glands and hormones' that were talking, it didn't change the fact that he felt he had to break with everything in his past. He wanted to burn all his bridges and start again from scratch and to really live.

Germaine, however, was distraught. Her life had been irrevocably entwined with that of her husband's for the past sixteen years and she loved him deeply, but her closest friends were also his, so this situation placed a great deal of stress on the whole group. Germaine would talk to Marcel Dehaye and Edgar Jacobs, as well as Hergé's father, Alexis Remi, about the problems she and Hergé were facing.

Hergé and Germaine decided to go on another trip together. They headed to Brittany at the end of August, but it was an unmitigated disaster.

Germaine wrote to Alexis Remi on 5 September, calling him 'Papa' and told him how sorry she was to send him bad news, but that nothing between her and Hergé was working any more, and they had decided to split up. She said that Brittany was beautiful, but she was having a terrible time.

At that time, she said that Hergé had not changed, and the whole situation was going from bad to worse. He was being nasty and cruel, and he had fits of anger. Despite all her courage, Germaine was at the end of her resistance and her nerve.

They returned to Paris from Brittany and separated, with Hergé leaving immediately for Switzerland to find his new love, but almost as soon as he met his mistress, he began writing to Germaine again. By 16 September, the affair was over.

Hergé realised that there were so many things that made the relationship between his new partner and himself difficult. She had a family, a husband and children, and she had been married for six years. He even listed her friends, lifestyle, education, and worries as things that stood in the way. And he understood that there were so many things that bound Germaine and him together. They had so many memories, both good and bad, and there were so many irreplaceable and priceless things they had shared.

In terms of work, although Hergé had been largely absent for a long while now, *Tintin* magazine was going from strength to strength. The magazine celebrated its second anniversary on 23 September, and due to its continued success, the number of pages would be increased to twenty. There would also be a French version launching on 24 October.

But there were more pressing concerns closer to home. Germaine was ill after struggling through all the turmoil of the year and had travelled to Bruges to take a much-needed break with her mother. Hergé needed to take a break too, and Marcel Dehaye had just the place in mind.

Chapter 12

Marcel Dehaye realised Hergé was in bad shape and persuaded him to take a rest in the truly peaceful place of the Trappist abbey of Scourmont near Chimay. It was here that Hergé met Father Gall, a monk who had a deep interest in the lives and culture of American Indians, and had even learned the Sioux language in order to write to the tribe.

Hergé was enchanted and the pair became good friends. On 12 October, Hergé wrote to Germaine to tell her of his experiences, in particular of Father Gall's den, which was at the top of a tower. He told her that when he was there, it was easy to forget he was in an abbey, and he felt he could be in a real Sioux tent. The den was adorned with all kinds of American Indian paraphernalia, such as eagle-feather headdresses, bows and arrows, tomahawks, guns, a peace pipe, and many more exciting objects – a paradise for the former Boy Scout.

He and Father Gall talked for a long time. They discussed people including Sitting Bull, Crazy Horse, Red Cloud, Spotted Tail, and all the famous Indian chiefs, as well as the battles in which they had made their names, such as Little Big Horn and Wounded Knee.

Father Gall delighted Hergé by showing him photos of his friends Black Elk and Little Warrior, and telling him their stories. He would also tell the cartoonist about his own life, and specifically that of his grandmother, who had almost married a Sioux man. Hergé boasted to Germaine that Father Gall was Sioux by adoption himself; he was actually part of the 'White Butte Band', which was a tribe of Ogallala Sioux.

Hergé spent the next day in the woods with Father Gall, who had dressed up as a Sioux chief, and they smoked the peace pipe together in a long, elaborate ceremony. He was in his element as he loved the culture of the American Indians, and it also brought back memories of his long, happy days in the Boy Scouts.

He wrote to Germaine on 12 October, to tell her how much he had been thinking. He said he had realised how lucky he had been, and now knew that life had smiled on him and given him everything he could have wished for and more. Above all, he had been given love. He was grateful for her, for his fame, health and comfort, even if he had not quite achieved wealth.

Suddenly aware of all he had, he knew he had everything a man could want, or he had at least tasted it. He had experienced enough fame to not want it to grow any more. He felt he had travelled enough to know that you cannot escape yourself, even at the other side of the world. He felt he had enough money to realise that objects and luxuries can never bring happiness, even after they have been desired and bought; he added that he had even driven enough cars to know that they are luxury toys, and he had had his fill of them.

She had given him absolutely everything, he told her, and she had filled him with joy. He wondered why he was now filled with such anxiety, why he was experiencing a deep dissatisfaction and feelings of uncertainty, and questioned why his life was lacking joy and enthusiasm.

He thought about everything, and felt in a vague, confused way that there was something else he was missing. He said he had an 'absolute need' he carried within himself, and always had a nagging suspicion that there was something else, something more important than anything, and this thought had reached a greater level of intensity than ever before. He said that was what was causing in him the detachment that Germaine mistook for a feeling of ingratitude toward life.

But it seemed as though a change was afoot. Hergé felt he had needed to suffer to know how much he was attached to Germaine and to appreciate what a wonderful woman she was. He now knew he understood her all the better and realised how much of his work he owed to her, as she had put herself in the background and sacrificed her own career and life to allow him to devote himself entirely to his drawing.

He also addressed the issue of children, which they rarely mentioned. He said that she had buried within herself the need and 'the thirst for a child that every woman carries within her'. Hergé told her that she had put him first there as well, thinking above all of his need for peace and quiet to complete his work.

The truth of the matter was that the couple were not able to have children, and it was a painful subject for the pair. Hergé had undergone radiation treatment in his younger days for a bad case of 'itching', which had rendered him sterile.

From time to time, the couple would talk of adopting a child, but never went any further with the plan, mainly because Hergé insisted on calm and quiet to focus on his comic strips, and a child would have thrown his cherished routine and peaceful environment into chaos. They would sometimes have Hergé's niece, Denise, to stay with them, but it was never long before he would become impatient with her.

After exchanging soul-baring letters for months concerning his current crisis, Hergé eventually returned to their house on the Avenue Delleur on the outskirts of Brussels, and tried to settle into a rhythm of work again. Marcel, with Germaine's help, had organised his new studio on the first floor and had arranged for his assistants to be on the floor above.

Hergé felt he was over his crisis and he and Germaine took up life together again, while he continued trying to work. When it was going well, he would whistle his favourite jazz tunes; when he struggled to concentrate, he would retreat outside and polish his Lancia.

He still wrestled with depression, which would manifest itself in a sudden onset of boils, as well as eczema on his hands, which would be so painful that it would stop him from drawing. He consulted a variety of doctors, but no one could find a solution.

Hergé had always been interested in alternative medicine, as well as astrology and the paranormal, so when his friend, Franz Jagueneau, suggested that his mother, Bertje, who marketed herself as a clairvoyant, might be able to help, Hergé jumped at the chance. Bertje met with Hergé and discussed a range of matters at length with him before she gave him her advice. She explained that he needed to change his diet and also advised him not to drink white wine. He diligently followed her advice and felt better almost immediately.

Hergé and Germaine stayed together and even went skiing for the first time that Christmas, as he was trying to live a more balanced, restful life.

After *Prisoners of the Sun* had finished in April 1948, the staff of *Tintin* magazine had re-serialised one of Hergé's old stories, *Popol and Virginia*, while he had taken his long break from work.

When he finally returned home, rested and renewed, he was ready to work again. Hergé wanted to create a story based around Tintin travelling to the moon, but Germaine and Marcel Dehaye suggested bringing back *Land of Black Gold*, an older story that had been interrupted by the war, and finishing that instead. This would mean less work for Hergé, who was still in a fairly fragile state, and would hopefully cause him less stress. Hergé took their advice and so work started on *Land of Black Gold*.

The first half had appeared in *Le Petit Vingtième* eight years earlier in 1940. The story began again in *Tintin* magazine on 16 September 1948, but Hergé decided to start the story from scratch, rather than continue from the point where it had ended rather abruptly.

He repaired the comic strip and inserted the new characters that had been introduced since then, such as Captain Haddock and Professor Calculus, as well as Marlinspike Hall.

Hergé's contract with the magazine stated that he was obliged to produce two pages of comic strips for each issue. In the previous story of *Prisoners of the Sun*, he had fulfilled this by supplying two pages of new Tintin stories every week. This time he was conscious of trying to make his workload more manageable, and decided to create only one new page per week of *Land of Black Gold*, while the other page was filled with stories from an old series of *Jo, Zette and Jocko*.

However, by 4 August 1949, Hergé had once again become ill and felt unable to work. The story was on hold, and the magazine hid the truth of Hergé's ill-health. Instead they used it as a publicity stunt with the headline in the next issue reading, 'Shocking news: Hergé has disappeared!', to create a mystery for their young readers.

But Hergé was struggling – with work and with married life. He and Germaine were constantly at odds with each other. She left for Paris, while he visited Gland in Switzerland again, as had become his usual habit in times of stress.

He wrote to Germaine on 5 August 1949, examining the turmoil they had been through the previous year. He said he had wanted to be free, and had seen himself on the Colorado River or sailing for Buenos Aires on a cargo ship. He was attracted by the idea of the different ports of call, the palm trees and a girl in every port. He had imagined himself a 'combination of Livingstone and Casanova'. But he said the worst aspect of his crisis was that he had taken it all so seriously, and of course, Germaine had inevitably done so, too.

Hergé realised how much drama he had caused and said he had 'fought and shouted' and had drowned himself in being tragic. He felt he had been overwhelmed with fatigue, and said that his brain hadn't been working properly. He was tired and in desperate search of rest, and had just needed to remove himself from work and drop all responsibilities and worries.

The major problem the couple had at the time was that for Hergé, Germaine was inextricably associated with work. After all, they had met at work, she constantly helped him with his job and they even had the work studio within their house. For someone wanting to escape from their job, he found it difficult to be around her.

While he was still struggling with work and his marriage, he nevertheless wrote to Dehaye on 10 August to say that at least his 'sentimental-erotic crisis is over' and that 'Don Juan-ism' was no longer for him.

Edgar Jacobs offered some robust analysis and advice for his friend on 16 August. He wrote to Hergé to try to shake him out of his melancholic state, telling him it seemed as though he was trying to put on a little show, almost in spite of himself. He wanted his friend to grow up, and told him that the problems he was talking about were 'the sorts of questions people ask themselves when they are between eighteen and twenty years old – the romantic period.'

He added, 'What you are going through is perfectly human, and all these feelings (whatever Germaine says) are a matter of temperament... So, go! Flit and flutter from flower to flower! But don't rush forward like a big bumblebee hitting a window-pane!'

Jacobs had had enough of waiting for Hergé to return to his responsibilities and did not mince his words. He told him that it was clear Hergé wanted to remain at any price the 'Big Man' that Germaine had wanted him to be, and it was also clear that he seemed to have forgotten that there was a man lying dormant in him, alluding to his numerous affairs.

He told Hergé that he was afraid of his work and that he flinched away from responsibility, just as his reputation was beginning to reach its peak. He wrote:

'Wake up, old fellow! You've been spineless for long enough. You need to shake yourself and get back on the horse; an artist, no matter how highly thought of he may be, is quickly forgotten once he's off the scene. You are responsible for the life of a newspaper that has a great deal of influence over young people, and that has the support and the ear of an even larger part of the public. You have to be confident in yourself – the thing has been launched in France and Italy – and at the end of the day there are two or three dozen people depending on you. I have the vague impression that you aren't conscious of the success and the fantastic luck that have marked your career. If you spent a couple of years as a starving artist, you'd sing a very different tune. What more can you want, for the love of God! You have fame, wealth, and youth!'

He ended the brusque letter with:

'And get it through your head that there are two things that matter in life; money and health! That's all. Anything other than that is gravy. No work – no money; no money – no 'little Switzerland'...'

Hergé was still unconvinced and reluctant to return to work. Germaine felt that Hergé's trips to Switzerland indicated he needed a more balanced lifestyle, with more nature and more exercise. She suggested buying an old farmhouse in Céroux-Mousty, Brabant, and Hergé was keen. They started the process of buying the property. He asked Germaine to come and visit him in Gland, Switzerland, and she travelled down in September, where they spent time with friends, eating and rowing. But he was still not keen to come back to Brussels to work on the magazine.

By now, even Marcel Dehaye was becoming frustrated with Hergé and urged him to let them know when they could expect the next instalment of Tintin. He also encouraged the cartoonist to talk frankly with Raymond Leblanc, who he suspected was becoming increasingly angry at Hergé's frequent absences. Hergé took his friend's advice and returned to Brussels in time for a dinner to celebrate the third anniversary of the *Tintin* magazine.

The Adventures of Tintin started to appear in the magazine again on 27 October. Hergé had taken twelve weeks off, and the magazine showed their feelings about this with the cover of the latest issue, which depicted a handcuffed Hergé dragged back to work by his characters. Thomson says to him, 'Enough laughter, my boy! Back to work!'

And with that, Hergé was back at the drawing board, working on *Land of Black Gold* until it was finally finished.

Raymond Leblanc had been very unhappy with Hergé's absences and he wished that the magazine could do without him. He felt they couldn't rely on the cartoonist as he had broken a string of promises to the editor. However, the magazine was still doing well and the pair had a contract together, so they had to remain cordial. The editor suggested that he should hire some more staff to take the burden off Hergé. While Hergé was keen to give away the more mundane technical jobs, he did not want an industrial, conveyor belt-style studio.

Now he was back, Hergé was keen to regain control. He had been very unhappy with the work of Andre Fernez, who had taken over from Van Melkebeke, and did not keep his feelings to himself. He criticised everything he had done for the magazine, and made life difficult for Fernez.

The artists on staff had now grown from the original four of Hergé, Jacobs, Laudy and Cuvelier to include Etienne Le Rallic and then Jacques Martin, followed by Willy Vandersteen and Bob De Moor.

Hergé was not one to pull any blows when it came to work and harshly criticised the efforts of most of the artists under him, bar Cuvelier, whom he felt a strong affinity with. He would have long talks with Cuvelier, who was also disenchanted with the medium of comic strips. Cuvelier looked at his work as just a job, but he had lofty ambitions to be much more and Hergé could empathise.

Chapter 13

Now *Land of Black Gold* was finished, Hergé could move on to a new story and he had plans to send Tintin to the moon in another double book adventure. He and his collaborators had been knocking the idea back and forth for a long time now. While he had been in crisis mode in Switzerland in the summer of 1948, he had confirmed to Marcel Dehaye that there would indeed be a new story and he had asked his collaborators to help.

Jacques Van Melkebeke and Bernard Heuvelmans had been working on a few ideas, which at the time Hergé had looked over with little more than apathy. Fast-forward to 1949 and the story had been through a series of revisions, and Hergé now used the work created by others to start his own story.

While Hergé ignored much of the development documents prepared by his staff and went in a different direction entirely, he did use some of the ideas word for word. However, when Heuvelmans would come to him many years later in 1962 asking for money to supplement the salary he had been paid at the time for his 'scriptwriting duties', Hergé robustly knocked him back, telling him there was no question of Jacques Van Melkebeke and Heuvelmans being scriptwriters of the story. While admitting that he had used some of the jokes they had suggested, as well as the scientific material, he firmly rejected the idea that they had come up with the scenario.

By November 1949, he firmed up Heuvelmans' role and asked him to gather various documents concerning technical aspects of space exploration, such as pictures of atomic factories, lunar rockets and the interiors of spaceships, as if to ensure his staff knew exactly what was expected of them – no more filling in for the boss.

Fascinated by the thought of human space travel, which was a feat that had yet to be achieved, Hergé wanted extensive research into the area for the drawings to be as realistic as possible.

He also wanted to employ another assistant to help with the new story, and although Jacques Van Melkebeke had just been released from jail, Hergé did not employ his friend. Instead he brought in Albert Weinberg, who had studied law and then worked for various cartoonists. He would eventually create the Dan Cooper pilot stories for *Tintin* magazine.

Hergé requested that Weinberg help with the new project and also asked him to create the basic framework for his next story, *Explorers on the Moon*. They would meet at Hergé's house and discuss the matter in detail, with Weinberg charged with the responsibility of finding ideas to fill out the story.

As a dutiful assistant, Weinberg helped Hergé with panels and gave suggestions, which Hergé took and used in his own inimitable way, condensing the material and restructuring extensively.

Hergé loved the topic of the new story and was in his element. He contacted Alexandre Ananoff, the Russian–French space expert, writing to him on 18 April 1950 asking for specific details of the instruments within the cockpit of a spaceship, especially their names and functions. Ananoff was keen to help Hergé in any way possible as he wanted children to be given accurate information on this subject.

After visiting the Center for Atomic Research of the ACEC, Hergé also contacted the director, Max Hoyaux. He immersed himself in the subject, bought a great number of books and became somewhat of an expert on space. His ultimate aim was to add a layer of accuracy never seen before in comic strips and he loved the challenge.

Working all hours on the new adventure, Hergé and his team eventually came up with the story of *Destination Moon*. The new instalment began in *Tintin* magazine on 12 March 1950 and ran until September of that year before being published by Casterman in 1953. The story revolves around Tintin and Captain Haddock, who are invited to Syldavia by Professor Calculus, where he is working on a confidential government project to send an astronaut to the moon. The story was a technical work of art and the readers loved the adventure and the meticulous drawings.

Over the duration of this project, there was a great shift in the way Hergé worked. On 6 April 1950, Studios Hergé public corporation was created, giving Hergé the technical support he needed. Hergé added

Arthur Van Noeyen to his stable of artists and asked his friend Jacques Van Melkebeke to train him up.

To further separate work from home life, the Studios were now based in his Avenue Delleur house in Brussels, with Hergé making the newly-purchased country house in Céroux-Mousty his and Germaine's main home. The Studios system now meant that Hergé had his own official team to help him with ongoing projects. He took on Bob De Moor as his primary apprentice at the Studios in March of the following year.

There were also great changes within Belgium itself. Since the end of the war, King Leopold III had been exiled in Switzerland with his second wife, Princess Lilian de Rethy, and his children. He had met with Hergé and formed a friendship while abroad, but desperately wanted to return to his homeland to resume his position as king and take over from his brother, Prince Charles, who was acting as regent in his absence.

A public referendum decided his fate in which citizens were asked to answer the question, 'Do you believe that King Leopold should resume the exercise of his constitutional powers?'

The public were divided, and although the results were in his favour, with 57.68% answering 'yes', the people who voted 'no' were in a majority in Brussels and in Wallonia, which greatly upset Leopold. Nevertheless, he returned home on 22 July 1950, but there were protests in Wallonia in which four people were killed and more protests were planned for Brussels itself. King Leopold III felt he had no choice but to abdicate, passing over the throne to his son, Baudouin.

Hergé was incredibly disappointed for his friend. On 15 May 1950, he was dealt another blow. His contact at Casterman Publishing, Charles Lesne, who had been an enormous part of Hergé's professional life for many years and had also become a friend and mentor, died suddenly of a heart attack.

Louis Casterman was moving away from the day-to-day tasks, so Hergé was left to deal with Casterman's son, Louis-Robert, who was not interested in Hergé's new ideas – his only concern was to keep the book sales high.

Although there were many changes, work was going well for Hergé. But towards the end of the summer, he began to feel very tired again, and by the time *Destination Moon* finished in September of that year, he was exhausted.

The story was planned as a double book, with a narrative that spanned two volumes, but rather than continue the weekly instalments, the adventure stopped abruptly in *Tintin* magazine – with the simple announcement: 'End of part one'.

Hergé was suffering from another bout of depression, and left again for his bolthole in Gland, Switzerland, with Germaine. He was exhausted by even the smallest things, and suddenly developed a fear of the water. While he had previously loved to swim and row, he was now gripped with terror upon entering the lake.

In many ways he was worse than before, and couldn't even complete letters to his friends. Germaine would have to take over a letter to Marcel telling him that Hergé was exhausted and that even a short trip to Geneva had left him in pieces. She said he needed around six months to properly recuperate.

Meanwhile, although they had bought the farmhouse in Ceroux as a family home, hoping it would offer Hergé the tranquillity he needed, the house needed a great deal of building work and was currently undergoing a renovation which only served to add to Hergé's stress and anxiety.

They returned to Brussels at the end of September, but he was still unable to work. Abbot Wallez had been released from jail and came to visit the couple for a few weeks. He had recovered from his illness, and although he was weak, he managed to be very vocal. During his stay, he would discuss the unfairness of the Purge, the accusations, the war and the subsequent war trials at great length, which did nothing to settle Hergé's already frayed nerves.

By February 1951, Hergé was struggling to cope. He wrote to his friend Paul Jamin, who was still in jail, waiting to be released, to tell him how he was feeling. He told him that he had been, and still was, extremely groggy. He said that he was suffering from overwork, with shredded nerves, awful insomnia, and attacks every time he made the mistake of sitting down at his work table.

He told his friend he had had to interrupt his stories in the magazine many times, and he felt that each time he had returned to work too soon, but this time he wouldn't be starting work until he felt completely well again.

The country house had been another huge source of concern. Bought for peace and relaxation, the property had been a millstone around their neck. The house had needed extensive renovations, which had caused a huge amount of stress.

In the same letter, he told Jamin that he was shocked the entire house hadn't collapsed yet, and he thought it could still happen. The developer had assured Hergé that the remodelling work would be done in six weeks. So far, it had been nearly a year since the work had started.

In the meantime, he said the costs were mounting fast: 'The bills come with the speed of machine-gun fire. *Boom!* The joiner's bill. *Blam!* The plumber's! *Pow!* The architect's! I've already spent a huge sum on architects; I've had to show two of them the door…'

Work was still halted on the *Explorers on the Moon* story, upsetting more and more readers. On 18 April 1951, Hergé wrote a letter to be printed in the magazine to address the issue and to provide an explanation for the absence of their favourite comic strip, saying:

'*Dear reader,*

I don't really know how to apologise for the long interruption of Explorers on the Moon. *I have been telling you in pictures the adventures of Tintin, Milou (Snowy), and all their companions; and of Jo, Zette, and Jocko, and of Quick and Flupke, for more than twenty years. But though all of those rascals are tireless, unfortunately I am not like them!*

Do you realize how much work is involved in a picture-story like the ones that appear in this magazine? Tell yourself that the cartoonist must be scriptwriter, decorator, costume designer, dialogue writer, and even sometimes actor (right, Edgar Jacobs?) all at the same time. He must also educate himself from books, journals, illustrated weeklies, and sometimes even actual places!

Imagine to yourself that all of this means research, reflection, and continuous work, and you will see that the job of "storyteller in images" is not a job that leaves time for any rest.'

He added that he had been ill and that doctors had recommended he take time off to rest, illustrating the letter with a picture of himself flopped in an armchair. Hergé was the only cartoonist of his time to place himself in the public eye in this way. He was also searingly honest in his replies to readers who asked where Tintin had gone and explained why he couldn't work.

Hergé had added Bob De Moor to his stable of artists in Studios Hergé on 6 March 1951. De Moor had previously worked for the Flemish version of *Tintin* magazine called *Kuifje*, but even having this fast, competent addition to the team did not help matters. Still Hergé was not ready to work.

The relationship with Leblanc and other members of the team was becoming increasingly strained. Marcel Dehaye wrote to Hergé on 18 December 1951, to say that he, Jacobs and other colleagues and friends were disappointed with the way he was acting. He told him that he should either retire completely or stand with them so that they could succeed. They were asking him to be loyal to the ideals that he himself had conceived. Dehaye implored him to return by telling him that there was nothing more disappointing than seeing a master fall short, and that was what he was forcing them to experience.

Whether it was Dehaye's impassioned request or all the rest and recuperation, Hergé finally decided to go back to work, and the Tintin story resumed in the magazine on 9 April 1952 with a summary of the story so far. The series continued to appear regularly until the end of the tale on 4 February 1953, much to everyone's relief.

However, it was just a short time after he returned to work that disaster struck. Hergé had an eye for cars and enjoyed driving at speed. While driving his beloved Lancia in the countryside with Germaine on 17 February 1952, he had gone to overtake a slower driver and the other car had tried to turn left down a country road. The cars smashed into each other and Germaine held her leg and cried out in agony.

They waited for the emergency services on the road for nearly an hour and a half before Germaine was taken by ambulance to Ottignies hospital, and from there she was taken to the Solbosch clinic in Brussels where she was given an X-ray. This revealed a bad fracture, with terrible bone splinters everywhere. Hergé told his friend that Germaine's bone had literally burst under the impact of the car crash.

The operation took place the next Wednesday and went well. A steel rod was inserted into the bone to ensure her leg would be the same length as the other one, and doctors assured Germaine that she wouldn't limp.

The day after the operation, Germaine developed a high fever, and for the next few days her heartbeat was irregular. They were both scared and Hergé thought the worst was going to happen to his wife, but she survived.

With a large cast on her leg, Germaine had to remain in hospital for weeks. Eventually, she was able to return home, but she was frustrated with her slow recovery. Abbot Wallez wrote to wish her well, and she was glad to receive his letter. But in another blow for the couple, he was also unwell and passed away on 24 September 1952. The pair were distraught at his death as he had meant so much to both of them.

Germaine was wheelchair-bound for months on end. She eventually started to walk again, but did so with a limp. She was extremely unhappy and blamed Hergé for her dire situation. The clairvoyant who had cured Hergé of his eczema, Bertje Jagueneau, would spend many afternoons with Germaine and the pair grew very close, with the former claiming to tell Germaine's horoscope. She would also concoct remedies to help her manage her pain. Germaine began to drink heavily.

Jagueneau wanted to deal with the renovation of the house in the countryside for the couple. She would also influence Hergé on his friendships, particularly in regard to Jacques Van Melkebeke, whom she regarded as a bad egg. Van Melkebeke would later write: 'Hergé ended his friendship with me, a Dutch clairvoyant having told him that my 'aura' had a deleterious influence on him.'

Another of Hergé's colleagues, Bernard Heuvelmans, was also surprised by the couple's friendship with Jagueneau, and saw the arguments with Van Melkebeke first hand. On one occasion, Hergé and Germaine had the Van Melkebekes and Jagueneau over to their house. Van Melkebeke would make sarcastic jokes, which Jagueneau did not like at all. She would criticise him and then told him, 'You are a bad influence on Georges; I see it, I feel it; you are evil.'

Shortly after that evening, Hergé ended his friendship with Van Melkebeke. He had had a great relationship with the man, but he believed what Jagueneau said.

However, Hergé's friendship with Van Melkebeke had already been strained after the Purge. It had been a bone of contention that they had both created similar work during the Occupation, but Hergé had emerged from the whole affair much less tainted than Van Melkebeke, who had spent time in prison for his actions.

Germaine had also been worried about Van Melkebeke's influence on Hergé and was not keen on their friendship. Van Melkebeke and his wife, Ginette, had a fiery relationship, with both of them often having affairs. Germaine was concerned about the effect they had on her husband, given the way he had acted over the last few years.

As Germaine suffered with her injuries from the car crash and friendships fell apart, Hergé floundered, but rather than escaping as he had been prone to do over the previous few years, this time he threw himself into work instead. He became more and more involved in the magazine, and also wanted to help out his old friends.

It was during the 1950s that many of Hergé's friends and former colleagues were released from jail, and Hergé wanted to look after them as much as he could, possibly feeling guilty at the lenient treatment he had experienced when they had been dealt with much more harshly. Many of them were unable to continue working in their former profession legally, and Hergé gave them work and let them write under pseudonyms, which was a risky course of action in that period.

Robert Poulet, the journalist and Nazi collaborator, said the day after Hergé died:

> *'I can say it now: between 1950 and 1960, he was the guardian angel of the "inciviques", the great supporter of the execrated and the banned whom he knew to be completely honest. My friend Georges, I want to acknowledge here, did so many things for me, and many others, when times were most difficult for us…I am, and will remain, always morally in his debt, and am bound to him by an unshakeable brotherhood of the heart.'*

Raymond Leblanc, on the other hand, was furious when he found out what Hergé had been doing. He later commented on the help Hergé had given to these people, saying:

> '*Eventually, that fucking Hergé surrounded me – without warning me – with a knot of former collaborators! And he went even further; Robert Poulet, who had been sentenced to death in absentia, actually wrote for Tintin under Hergé's protection. Poulet's wife lived in Brussels and came to my office, passing herself off as the author of texts her husband had actually written for us. This lasted a long time.*'

Indeed, when Raymond De Becker, the former editor of the 'pirate' *Le Soir*, was freed, Hergé wanted to hire him for the magazine, but De Becker was no longer allowed to work as a journalist. Instead he worked under the name of 'Pierre Marinier'. Hergé loaned De Becker money and set him various projects to work on.

As Leblanc slowly began to realise what was happening, he would start to quiz anyone suggested for a position by Hergé about their legal standing. Regardless, the magazine during this period was often thought of as a 'nursery for collaborators'.

After he returned to work on a regular basis, Hergé sought to reassert himself within the publication. In 1952, he wanted to modernise *Tintin* magazine and make it more topical and current, with lively features and scientific articles. He was very keen to reinsert current events into the magazine, despite all the problems this had caused for him in the past. He also wanted the cartoonists to develop their own style and to be more experimental, despite training them formally in his own strict methods. Hergé was back and he was in charge.

Chapter 14

By 1953, Hergé had made many changes to his life. Due to Germaine's injury, they had had to move from their house on Avenue Delleur to a small apartment in a building with a lift. They were now on the Rue de Livourne, set opposite Marcel Dehaye and crucially, a short distance from Studios Hergé, which he had moved from his house to Avenue Louise.

Hergé had finally managed to strike a balance and separate his work from his personal life. He and Germaine would stay in the apartment during the week, where Hergé would work for fixed hours, and then they would retreat to the country house, which was finished after the extensive renovation, for the weekends.

Business was going well and the relationship between Leblanc and Hergé, which had been strained by the latter's frequent absences over the past few years, was now peaceful again.

The Studios employed three new members of staff, and the first was Baudouin van den Branden de Reeth. He came from a prestigious family who were friends with the monarchy and he was a former classmate of Bernard Heuvelmans. Baudouin became Hergé's secretary, while Baudouin's wife, Jacqueline, was made the editorial secretary for *Tintin* magazine.

Baudouin van den Branden de Reeth had moved in similar circles to Hergé and he knew him fairly well. His friend Raymond De Becker, the former editor of the pirate *Le Soir*, imprisoned for his work during the Occupation, had been deeply in love with Baudouin for years, but his love was unrequited.

Baudouin and Hergé became close friends, and would often meet at the Studios on a Saturday morning just for a quiet talk. He was a wilder character than Hergé – when they travelled to Paris together, Baudouin suggested they could visit a brothel and Hergé was rendered speechless!

The secretary's new duties included reviewing dialogue in the comic strips and answering letters from readers, as well as generally helping Hergé.

The second person to be recruited for the Studios was Jacques Martin, who had previously worked on *Tintin* magazine from his base in Paris. Hergé eventually persuaded him to move to Brussels to join his close-knit team.

The third addition to the Studios team was Josette Baujot, a cartoonist and widow from Argentina, who would be in charge of the coloration detail for over twenty-five years. Hergé was unaccustomed to dealing with women, and when Baujot commented on her salary not being high enough, he replied, 'All the same, it's not bad for a woman!' which was not received well. His treatment of women was also criticised years later, when Baudouin van den Branden de Reeth was unable to work and his wife took over his job, for which Hergé paid her two-thirds of her husband's former salary.

Although Hergé had managed to put together a strong team of experts, time was ticking on and still a new Tintin story had yet to appear. Previous stories such as *Prisoners of the Sun* and *Land of Black Gold* had mainly involved rehashing and finishing old stories, while the moon-based adventures had been conceived just after the war. Hergé wanted something current and exciting for his next comic strip.

Inspiration struck when he read an article in the Belgian weekly *La Face à Main* in February 1954, and Hergé was moved to start the next adventure. The story concerned a strange series of incidents in the UK. Over the previous three years, there had been sixty-seven accidents affecting drivers on the road from Portsmouth to London. At a certain point along the road, and always in the same place, the windshield of their cars would break, and no one had ever discovered the cause.

It had been revealed that 300 metres from the place where these accidents had occurred was a top-secret facility where special instruments converted electrical energy into concentrated ultrasonic sound waves, which produced sounds that were inaudible to the human ear but were capable of piercing holes in steel plates. The police had never been allowed to enter the facility, but the report questioned whether the mysterious sound waves were the cause of the windshield breakages.

Hergé was fascinated by the story, and so, assisted by Jacques Martin, he began *The Calculus Affair*.

The story follows the attempts of Tintin, Snowy and Captain Haddock to save Professor Calculus, who had developed a machine capable of destroying objects with sound waves, from being kidnapped by the rival European countries of Borduria and Syldavia.

Reflecting the Cold War tensions of the 1950s, *The Calculus Affair* came at a time when espionage thrillers were very popular in both France and Belgium.

The new adventure began in *Tintin* magazine during December 1954, and introduced new characters into the world of Tintin. The first was the overbearing Jolyon Wagg, a Belgian insurance salesman, who appeared in each subsequent adventure apart from *Tintin in Tibet*. Also introduced was Cutts the butcher and chief of the Bordurian secret police, Colonel Sponsz.

Hergé was again keen to keep a sense of accuracy in the story, and after reading the article that influenced the plot, he consulted Professor Armand Delsemme, an astrophysicist in Liège, about the scientific elements he wanted to include in the adventure. He also wanted to present Switzerland accurately and contacted Jean Dupont, the editor of *L'Écho Illustré* in Switzerland which also serialised *The Adventures of Tintin*. He asked him to send pictures of Swiss railways so he could copy them exactly.

He also travelled to Switzerland to create sketches of areas around Geneva for the story, such as Geneva Cointrin International Airport and Genève-Cornavin railway station, as well as the Cornavin Hotel.

In a nod to Walt Disney, Hergé named a character Topolino, as Mickey Mouse was known as this in Italy. He also included a reference to his friend and colleague Edgar Jacobs, by adding a character named 'Jacobini' to the billing on the opera show alongside Bianca Castafiore, as well as including a cameo of himself as a reporter in the final scene.

The Calculus Affair began in *Tintin* magazine's Christmas edition on 22 December 1954 and continued to appear regularly until 22 February 1956. It was the first Tintin adventure to be printed without interruption since *Red Rackham's Treasure*, and is widely seen as Hergé's masterpiece and one of his best creations due to the vibrant illustrations and strong storyline.

Hergé was nearly fifty years old and felt thoroughly refreshed and energised. He was enjoying his work again and after he had finished *The Calculus Affair*, he started to think about the next project, but was keen to give himself a manageable workload. He wanted to take two or three months to find the basis for a new book and research the idea, and then planned to complete a page per week of the sixty-two-page story.

While he was working on the new idea, Hergé would often smoke. He had tried to quit smoking on two or three occasions, but these had ended in failure and he felt his willpower wasn't strong enough to keep him away from tobacco. He also smoked when he was unhappy or finding work difficult, and if he couldn't think of any new ideas or come up with a drawing, he would give in to temptation. It was often a sign to his colleagues that work was not going well.

But the Studio system was running smoothly. They were a close team and even Hergé's father would help out. He came to work at the Studios every afternoon and would help organise and file the reams of documents that the Studios amassed in their quest for accuracy.

While looking for inspiration for the new instalment of Tintin, Hergé had come across a magazine article about the slave trade in the Middle East, where it was claimed that African pilgrims heading to Mecca were being enslaved during the journey, and this led him to develop the new Tintin story entitled *The Red Sea Sharks*.

Hergé had also been reading Balzac's *The Human Comedy*, as well as books about the author, such as *Balzac and His World* by Félicien Marceau, and he was inspired by the way the author would reuse characters from his previous stories and sought to implement this in his new adventure.

The Red Sea Sharks began appearing in *Tintin* magazine in October 1956. The story follows Tintin, Snowy and Captain Haddock as they travel to Khemed with the aim of helping the Emir Ben Kalish Ezab regain control of the country after a coup by his opponents, who were backed by a group of slave traders.

In the style of Balzac, Hergé brought back numerous characters from past stories such as General Alcazar, Oliveira da Figueira, Dr Müller, Roberto Rastapopoulos and Jolyon Wagg. He also introduced a new character, the Estonian pilot Piotr Skut, who would also appear in the later *Flight 714 to Sydney*.

Once again keen to keep a degree of realism in his work, Hergé went even further than he had in previous stories. To provide accurate drawings of the Ramona steamer ship, Hergé and his assistant Bob De Moor travelled aboard a Swedish cargo vessel, the MS *Reine Astrid*, from Antwerp to Gothenburg and back, where they spent their time taking photos and sketching.

Hergé had also been collecting press cuttings, and used photos of the *Christina*, a motor yacht owned by the Greek shipping magnate Aristotle Onassis, as the basis for the drawings of Rastapopoulos's ship, the *Sheherezade*. Similarly, the drawing of the Emir's hideaway palace cut out of the rock was based on a picture of Al Khazneh in Petra, Jordan, from an issue of *National Geographic* magazine. As he developed an interest in modern art, Hergé was also keen to include this passion in the story and so paintings by Pablo Picasso and Joan Miró adorn the *Scheherazade* ship.

The cartoonist had faced many accusations of racism from previous stories, and in particular he had been vilified for his portrayal of Africans in one of his early adventures, *Tintin in the Congo*. With *The Red Sea Sharks*, he hoped to vindicate himself with a story that centred around his heroes Tintin and Haddock freeing African slaves. He was desperate not to offend people again and in preparation for the story, he consulted a friend who worked for an African-themed magazine, *Africa and the World*, and asked them to translate some of the text into the language spoken in West Africa, Yoruba.

However, despite his good intentions, the comic strip was criticised in various publications, including the magazine *Jeune Afrique*, for the racist depiction of Africans. The writers condemned the characters' simple use of pidgin language, which was very similar to the language style seen in *Tintin in the Congo*. Hergé was upset by the criticism, and changed the book for the reprint in 1967 by improving the grammar in the Africans' speech patterns.

Overall, the story was received very positively. It was seen as a reunion for the people in the Tintin world, with so many former characters appearing in the adventure. It was unusual in that it had a retrospective quality, and in many ways seemed to be a continuation of *Land of Black Gold*. Readers loved the complex nature and more adult theme of slavery in the story and deemed it to be a great thriller, and one of the best Tintin adventures.

Hergé was happy, and the studio system he had set up was working well. He could now give himself the luxury of more free time, which he spent going to the theatre and the cinema, but his main passion was reading – particularly books by Dickens and Proust, as well as Balzac.

Although he hadn't yet taken up painting as he had often discussed during his crisis period, he was becoming more and more interested in contemporary art. He had previously disliked abstract art intensely, but at this point he replaced a landscape painting he had by a great Flemish painter with one by Joan Miro, having developed a love of modernism. He would also spend weekends in his country pile, walking, gardening, playing the guitar or indulging in a game of table tennis or petanque.

In many ways, his life was idyllic. However, Hergé's relationship with Germaine had soured even further. She had not completely recovered from the accident, and as the Studio had moved out of the family home, her role within Hergé's work, which she had helped him with for so long, had diminished and she now had no great focus to take her mind off matters. She was bored and lonely, and blamed Hergé for her injuries.

Hergé also struggled in his relationship with his brother, Paul. After spending five years in a German prisoner of war camp, he had emerged as a war hero, but the experience had affected him greatly. Paul was now prone to drinking too much and became very outspoken, which harmed his career in the military. As he floundered, Hergé only became more and more successful.

While Hergé tried to help Paul on occasion, he was also critical of his brother, particularly in the way he brought up his two children, Denise and Georges. Hergé even suggested adopting the pair as he was so concerned about the family environment they were growing up in, but their mother categorically refused.

Denise would later say that Hergé and Germaine's proposal to adopt them had come as a surprise as she and her brother had never been keen to spend time with their aunt and uncle, who they had always found rather cold and distant. She added that they weren't a couple who attracted children, and that they could be quite critical. Denise had written to her uncle from her boarding school and twice he had replied simply imitating her childish handwriting and poor punctuation.

When Denise and Georges had visited Hergé's country house, the children felt it was like a museum, as they weren't allowed to touch anything and had to be quiet. Denise's younger brother Georges asked to leave early on several occasions because he was so bored.

Despite problems in his personal life, Hergé's work was going well, and in 1955, Studios Hergé wanted to recruit another colourist. They placed an advert in *Le Soir*, specifically asking for a female colourist, and received over thirty applications. The applicants were interviewed and asked to do a short test to check the quality of their work. While many of the applicants proved to be talented colourists, one woman stood out and would change Hergé's life forever.

She was Fanny Vlamynck – twenty years old, very beautiful and she already had connections to the Studio group. Fanny had been in school with Paul Jamin's daughter and had also been recommended by Baudouin van den Branden de Reeth. She joined the team and initially expected to find Hergé to be a rather imposing, older figure and was taken aback when she met him for the first time.

She would later say she was surprised to find someone who was almost a young man in Hergé, someone who was very relaxed, with his shirt-sleeves pushed up, and she found him impressive. As a colourist, Fanny saw little of Hergé, but when she did meet him, she thought he was charming and kind, but a bit distant. He gave her the impression he was watching over things with humour and benevolence, but that he was always holding something back.

Hergé had also recruited another colourist, France Ferrari, who joined the team in November 1955 and worked under the leadership of Josette Baujot. Fanny and France became close, and Fanny would soon confide in her new friend that she was very much attracted to Hergé.

Fanny was keen to impress and she desperately wanted to improve her style, so she took night courses, studying at the Academie de Saint-Josse. She would stay late at the office, waiting for her course to start, and it was in these moments that she would begin to get to know Hergé, who also worked late.

They would talk more and more, before starting an affair the night before the bank holiday weekend in November 1956, where they confessed they would miss each other over the long weekend break.

Hergé later said in an interview, 'It was like a little miracle! I hadn't seen her much more often than any other Studios employee. But over time, I watched her work, I watched her live, I listened to her… I don't know how it happened, but it happened all on its own, little by little.'

Hergé and Fanny only confided in France Ferrari and Baudouin about their affair, but Jacques Martin found out about the couple and told the rest of the staff.

People were not pleased about the development, some openly showing their displeasure. Josette Baujot caught Hergé one evening and tried to talk to him. She said, 'Do you think this little girl would be so interested in you if you were a streetcar conductor?' Hergé replied flatly that he was not a streetcar conductor, and Josette did not mention the topic to her boss again.

Baudouin and his wife tried a different tactic. He talked to Fanny to try to stop the affair, but when this failed to stop the pair, he even brought his handsome nephew into the office to see if she would fall for him instead. This only resulted in upsetting Hergé, and caused a strained relationship between the two men for a while.

Germaine sensed something was happening. She was tired and depressed and knew that Hergé was being distant with her. She felt that things between them hadn't been this bad since Hergé's affair in Switzerland in 1948.

To help her recover from her accident and also to cheer herself up, Germaine had embarked upon a new hobby: ballroom dancing. She began to enjoy it more and more, partly because she met a man called Bob at the class. He was kind and gentle, and Germaine could relax with him. She felt the stark difference between Bob and Hergé as she had never felt so relaxed with her husband.

She felt she was attaching more importance to this new friendship than she should, but she couldn't help falling for this new man as he was tender and sweet to her. It affected her so much that Hergé was hard and severe, lacking any kind of tenderness. She felt he loved her, but only because she was useful to him.

The situation carried on until April 1957, with Germaine writing about it in her notebooks. She constantly compared the two men. She felt young again with Bob, saying their relationship was of an almost amusing purity, which was why she found it so moving and lovely. She felt as though she was twenty years old again when she was with him. On the other hand, life with Hergé was lacking. Germaine felt she was living with Hergé without actually knowing him. She found his nature complicated, egotistical and wildly imaginative, but wondered what he actually thought about. She felt she didn't know simple things about him. He was an enigma to her.

Later that month, it was Hergé's fiftieth birthday as well as the couple's twenty-fifth wedding anniversary. Hergé and Germaine went on a cruise to celebrate. They departed on 23 May from Anvers, travelling to Casablanca, Rabat, Oran, Alger, Palermo and Rome. Germaine was miserable, pining for Bob, while Hergé missed Fanny.

However, the trip was still a fairly successful break for the couple, as their relationship was temporarily on better terms, but this was not to last. Soon the barbed conversations and tense atmosphere returned.

Hergé's niece, Denise, stayed with the unhappy couple for the summer and they tried to hide their difficulties as best they could. Germaine wanted to go on another break with Hergé and suggested a trip to Ostende in October. Hergé agreed, but the trip wasn't enjoyable for either of them.

Germaine felt that Hergé only agreed to the trip out of duty rather than kindness, and he was indifferent and hard towards her. She felt sick, drained and confused. After a dreadful Saturday together, the situation came to a head and Germaine finally exploded at the hotel. She told Hergé that they couldn't go on this way and that she deserved more interest and kindness from him. He was thrown by her attack and didn't know what to do.

Chapter 15

It was November before Hergé summoned the courage to tell his wife that he was in love with someone else. Hergé and Germaine were in their country house when he finally opened up on the Saturday night.

He was friendlier than usual, which put Germaine on guard right away. He drew her near, asking her to stay close to him, and said he needed all her indulgence and understanding, before revealing that he and Fanny were in love.

Germaine was left cold by the revelation, but was not shocked as she had suspected something had been going on for some time now. She felt very detached from him.

It was a time of turmoil for both Hergé and Germaine, and while she was not surprised to learn he was having an affair, she was stunned to find out it was with someone from the Studios. And Hergé was torn – he wanted Fanny, but couldn't let Germaine go.

Although Germaine had received the news stoically, she soon fell into a deep depression, and stopped seeing her love interest from the ballroom dance class. Instead, she would consult clairvoyant Bertje Jagueneau, who told the distressed Germaine that everything would work out and that Hergé couldn't do without her. Germaine later realised that she had placed too much weight on Bertje's advice, which made the situation worse.

Hergé would say that Germaine had nothing more to say or give to him, whereas Fanny on the other hand, had everything to teach him and everything to reveal. Hergé said that if he chose Fanny, he would be 'coming alive again with someone young' and having a sweeter, more pleasant life, which Germaine suggested would be difficult for someone with 'such a joyless personality'. Hergé felt guilty and didn't know what to do. He became angry easily and incredibly difficult to live with.

He later said in an interview, 'The separation, the period when everything turned upside down, was real agony for me. I had someone, my wife, who had truly dedicated her life to me, and who I couldn't really reproach for anything.'

Hergé stayed away from home to avoid the inevitable arguments with Germaine as often as possible.

Meanwhile, although his marriage was falling apart and he was in the middle of another crisis, work was progressing well for Hergé. *The Adventures of Tintin* in French were selling over a million copies per year, and the books were in the process of being translated for other countries such as Spain, the UK and the Scandinavian countries.

However, Hergé was having frequent confrontations with the editor of *Tintin* magazine, Andre Fernez, who eventually submitted his resignation in March 1958, partly due to his regular run-ins with the cartoonist.

Fernez was succeeded by Marcel Dehaye and the business was going smoothly under the direction of Raymond Leblanc, so much so that the owner dreamed of moving premises. Leblanc wanted to construct a building near the central railway station in Brussels, the Gare du Midi. Hergé was dubious about the plan, but agreed to pay for one floor of the building as Leblanc was so enthusiastic.

The new building was opened on 13 September 1958, and became the headquarters of Editions du Lombard which published *Tintin* magazine, and featured a rotating neon sign of Tintin and Snowy on the roof.

Hergé was struggling in his personal life, but to the outside world, it seemed as though he had it all. He was fifty-one, worked in the city Studios during the week, retiring to his mansion in the countryside via his Porsche 1600 on the weekends, and his book sales were going from strength to strength.

Paris-Match wrote a feature on Hergé and Tintin, as did the *Times Literary Supplement*. Books about his creations were being prepared as well, such as *Le Monde de Tintin* (The World of Tintin). Indeed, Hergé and Tintin were becoming cultural icons and the offers flooded in. People wanted to put Tintin on the stage in theatre productions and on radio series. Records were also being made. There was a black and white animation of the books on French TV, and the idea of films was mooted again, with a couple of slightly disappointing versions being made.

To cash in on the success and take his mind off matters of the heart, Hergé threw himself into his work and set about finding a new adventure for Tintin. He considered heading back to the USA with a story involving the American Indians again and also considered a story centred around a legal error and Nestor, one of Marlinspike's occupants. Eventually he settled on another idea and a new direction entirely – Tintin was off to Tibet.

Hergé had briefly considered the idea before and the fact that Bernard Heuvelmans had written a book in 1955 which featured a chapter on the 'Abominable Snowman' may have sparked this interest again.

However, he needed to find a reason for Tintin to visit Tibet. He veered between a spy story and one centred around forged paintings, before settling on a tale about Zhang, his friend from the early years, who had helped him greatly with *The Blue Lotus*, and even featured in that story as the character 'Chang'. Many readers had asked to see him return to *The Adventures of Tintin*.

Hergé wanted this to be a new kind of adventure, a story stripped of all the traditional bells and whistles of the comic strip with no villains or weapons, just simply the struggle of man against himself and the hostile elements.

He also wanted to have Tintin encounter a yeti on his travels, and so he underwent a great deal of research into the geographical area and the yeti itself. There were no photos of the animal, but he decided there were lots of animals that had not yet been photographed, so this did not deter the cartoonist. In February 1958, he asked Heuvelmans to research the yeti for him, and Heuvelmans' wife, Monique Watteau, actually came up with a picture of the animal.

Hergé was interested in all the slightly marginal sciences and he was attracted to unexplained phenomena. He believed in things such as clairvoyance, telepathy, and premonitory dreams, which all appear in Tintin, and he treated them quite seriously. In *Tintin in Tibet*, for example, he features a levitating monk, and Heuvelmans felt he was using the phenomenon in a serious way, almost with deference, because he believed in it so profoundly.

During this period, Hergé was influenced by the writings of Carl Gustav Jung. After Raymond De Becker was freed from jail, he had sought psychoanalysis to heal himself and understand the journey he had been on. De Becker got in touch with Jung in 1951. Jung was now seventy-five years old and lived in a house overlooking Lake Zurich in Switzerland. He spoke to De Becker, invited him to his home on a few occasions and accepted him as a patient for a short while, before referring him to one of his pupils, Professor Franz Riklin.

De Becker quickly became absorbed in Jung's writings, and became an authority on his work. He was a great influence on Hergé, who also soon became engrossed in the work of Jung.

In July 1958, Hergé started the new Tintin story after months of research and deliberation, with *Tintin in Tibet* first appearing in *Tintin* magazine in September of that year. The story revolves around Tintin's search for his friend Chang Chong-Chen, who the authorities claimed had died in a plane crash in the Himalayas. Convinced Chang had survived, Tintin sets off across the Himalayas to Tibet with Snowy, Captain Haddock and the Sherpa guide Tharkey, and along the way they encounter the enigmatic Yeti. This instalment of the series differed from anything that came before, as it featured only a few characters, and there was no enemy to foil. The story also included many themes that fascinated Hergé, such as extrasensory perception and Tibetan Buddhism.

But as he began to draw, he had nightmare after nightmare. He was so affected by these awful dreams that he would write them down. On 22 July 1958, he described a dream where he was throwing snowballs at little girls, when all of a sudden there was no more snow, apart from a tiny drop left on a rock. He tasted it, but it tasted strange. He said he knew he had to climb higher to get more snow and went into a slanting tunnel dug into the rocks.

Snow and little girls would feature heavily in his dreams, possibly indicating the trouble he was having developing his story and also the difficult decision he had to face regarding Fanny and Germaine. His parents would also feature in his dreams, where he would often lose them, and Hergé noted that he was often attracted to women who were fragile and soft, just as his mother had been.

Hergé would analyse his dreams with Fanny, who would also discuss the long, similar dreams she had been having. Many of his dreams and nightmares were predominantly concerned with the colour white, eerie and foreboding imagery, and a sense of danger or imminent terror. Other dreams were very obvious in terms of where they had come from. In one dream he was with Germaine in his country house, when Fanny came in and sat on his lap. He wrote that he was very upset and placed a furtive kiss on Fanny's hand. She kissed him back, but he avoided the kiss. Fanny then told him a long story and totally ignored Germaine, while Hergé explained that the two were only friends.

Hergé had more and more frequent dreams concerning Germaine and Fanny. In one he hugged Germaine and called her his 'little wife', but realised that he meant the words for Fanny, and felt both 'furious and comforted'.

The dreams reflected the reality that Hergé was struggling with. The combination of his Catholic upbringing and his Boy Scout ethos caused him to feel incredibly guilty that he was now in love with another woman. He later said in an interview with Numa Sadoul, 'It meant turning upside down all my values, what a shock! This was a serious moral crisis. I was married and I loved someone else. Life seemed impossible with my wife, but on the other hand I had this scout-like idea of giving my word for ever. It was a real catastrophe. I was completely torn up. I was going through a time of real crisis and my dreams were nearly always white dreams. And they were extremely distressing.'

Hergé was in turmoil and Germaine was extremely unhappy as her husband tried to decide between her and his girlfriend, who was twenty-seven years younger than the cartoonist. Germaine became bitter and frequently lost patience with him.

His personal life was taking its toll and Hergé was finding it difficult to work again, so he decided to seek help to decipher his upsetting dreams. De Becker recommended he consult the Swiss psychoanalyst Professor Riklin as Jung would no longer accept any new patients.

On 8 May 1959, Hergé took the notes he had been keeping on his dreams for the past year and met with Professor Riklin in Zurich. The meeting disturbed Hergé as he was told to destroy the demon of purity inside him by Riklin, which he found shocking. Riklin had also told him that he had to stop working because he couldn't focus on his recovery and his work at the same time. However, Hergé felt he could not abandon this project and hung on to finish *Tintin in Tibet* despite all his anguish.

Hergé would later say that he learnt from the meeting with Riklin that he needed to accept not being immaculate. He said that he had to learn that good and evil coexist, that there can't be one without the other. He also took from the experience that he had to accept what Jung calls 'the process of individuation', and had to admit to himself the tendencies he had denied before now and projected on to others.

After much soul-searching, nightmares and psychoanalysis, Hergé decided to leave Germaine towards the end of May 1959. However, although the decision had been made, Hergé was not sure when they would physically move apart and there were frequent traumatic scenes between the couple. They would often argue about the most mundane subjects and conflict was a common occurrence.

While Germaine became more vocal in her criticism of her husband, Hergé tried to avoid the confrontation and would retreat, responding only in his vivid dreams. On one occasion, Germaine and Bertje Jagueneau were chatting in the living room in their house, while Hergé sat nearby, smoking and silent. Germaine said to him, 'Always these cigarettes! You smoke them one after the other. What a lack of willpower!' Bertje chimed in to tell Hergé he had always been a spoiled child and she wondered what he would have become had he not met Germaine. Hergé promptly left the room, only replying to Germaine in the dream he had that night which replayed the same incident, but with him responding, 'To hell with you and your willpower... to hell with you, you hear me?'

After his single session with Riklin, he had begun to read more into his dreams and saw that this had been an example of 'repression, immediately followed by dream release'.

Hergé continued to work on his latest story, which was in many ways an escape. The whiteness of some of the panels in the story showed a starkness that reflects the dreams he was having, but also freed him from having to use a host of other artists to add all the detail that had become one of the hallmarks of his stories over the past few years. The stripped-back style in many ways showed a return to the form of his early years, although it was more mature in tone. The new story also illustrated more of an appreciation of wildlife, which counterbalanced the wanton slaying of animals that proliferated in *Tintin in the Congo*.

Meanwhile, Fanny left her job at Studios Hergé in September 1959, and became a model for the Hirsch fashion house instead. However, this was not to last. Germaine, who was still very bitter about the separation, attended one of the fashion shows with Bertje Jagueneau and sat in the front row glaring at Fanny throughout the evening. Extremely embarrassed by this incident, Fanny moved to work in the window display department at the fashion house instead, but she would soon leave that position too.

Fanny's professional life was suffering and her relationship with Hergé had reached a plateau. Although he would take Fanny out every Friday night, he was still living with Germaine and had started telling his wife that it was perfectly normal to have a 'secondary wife', and that people had always done it.

Hergé wanted Germaine to understand that he couldn't end his relationship with Fanny, but he also wanted to keep their marriage, as they had been through so much together. Jacqueline and Baudouin tried to help the three come to an agreement where Hergé could keep both relationships, and while Fanny and Germaine were possibly willing at one point to try, Hergé retreated from this idea, concerned that it constituted cheating.

The three were in constant turmoil. Germaine would sometimes hunt the pair down when they were meeting for illicit liaisons in out-of-the-way hotels, as Fanny still lived with her parents and they were unable to meet at her house. Hergé contracted a duodenal ulcer in the autumn of 1959 from all the stress, and on 4 November, he spoke to Germaine and told her that he could no longer stand to live like this and that he was leaving.

On 25 November 1959, the last section of *Tintin in Tibet* featured in *Tintin* magazine, and the story was well received by critics and readers alike. The exceptional adventure is possibly the most mature in the Tintin series and shows a vulnerability rarely seen in comic strips of the time – and was reflective of the heartache that Hergé was going through as he created the story.

The adventure centres around the unbreakable bonds of friendship, illustrated in the many moving moments throughout, such as the emotional reunion of Tintin and his friend Chang, Captain Haddock's offer to sacrifice his life for Tintin's, and the sadness of the Yeti as he watches his friend leave. The powerful combination of incredible artwork and a poignant story make this one of the most touching books in the history of comic strips, and Hergé's favourite of all the Tintin stories.

While he had reached a pinnacle in his career, his personal life was stagnating. Although he had told Germaine he was leaving in November, over three months later in February 1960, Hergé was still there. He was finding the situation interminable and decided to go to Switzerland for a break with Fanny.

After a calm trip away from his chaotic personal life at home, he returned on 24 February, refreshed and ready to move on. He moved out of his and Germaine's family home and into the Hotel Brussels on Avenue Louise, but did not mention to his wife that this would be a permanent separation.

He stayed at the hotel until July, when he decided to rent a small apartment in Uccle. He had finally made a decision about his personal life after being in a relationship with the twenty-six-year-old Fanny for almost four years.

While divorce was legal in Belgium, there was still a stigma attached and Germaine was very much against taking this step. Hergé was keen to keep the details of their situation within their inner circle of friends and family, too, and he certainly did not want their separation publicised. He would only have their very close friends over to his house, and Germaine would still accompany him to public events. They would continue with this arrangement until they finally divorced seventeen years later.

Hergé still spent every Monday evening with Germaine and would do so for years, but she struggled to come to terms with the situation. She felt Bertje Jagueneau had not been as helpful in her time of need as she had once thought, and now felt naive for trusting and believing her when the clairvoyant had said that she and her husband would overcome the problems in their relationship.

Germaine also found that she herself had changed and she now saw through Jagueneau, who constantly complained to her about money issues. Germaine felt as though she had been duped by all those who were closest to her.

In 1960, Hergé was barely up to creating another Tintin adventure and called upon Michel Greg to help develop his story ideas, and they worked on a few different scenarios before abandoning the plans. It was towards the end of the year that they would come up with the next big idea for Tintin.

Chapter 16

During a typical tea break at Studios Hergé, Jacques Martin, Baudouin van den Branden de Reeth, Hergé and the rest of the team were discussing ideas for the next adventure, when Baudouin suggested creating a story where the characters did not leave their home at Marlinspike. And so, one of the quirkiest stories of the Tintin canon was born.

With this new instalment of the series, all the previous ideas and formulas would be thrown out in favour of something entirely new. *The Castafiore Emerald*, which started in *Tintin* magazine in July 1961, is the only Tintin book where the characters remain at Marlinspike Hall, Captain Haddock's family estate, for the entire story. Rather than the usual exploits of confronting dangerous criminals in far-flung countries, this plot is centred around a visit from opera sensation Bianca Castafiore, and the theft of her precious emerald.

Hergé always described the arrangement of Tintin, Captain Haddock and Calculus living together as 'savoir-vivre'; they used the art of good manners to live together as well as possible, and knew how to enjoy life to the full. However, in this story they threw the larger-than-life character of Bianca Castafiore into their delicate eco-system of savoir-vivre, and the characters were out of their element, which made for a rather spectacular and experimental adventure.

While Bianca Castafiore was a central character in this story and made a grand entrance into the world of Tintin, there would not be a flood of women following in her footsteps.

Hergé later said in an interview, 'If I created the character of a pretty girl, what would she do in this world where all the beings are caricatures? I love women too much to make caricatures out of them! And besides, pretty or not, young or not, women are rarely comic elements. Is it that the maternal side of women doesn't lend itself to laughter? It is indeed strange to realise that women are absent from many comic strip stories. Or if they are there, they are rarely funny.'

The Castafiore Emerald was the antithesis of the previous Tintin adventures, and in many ways similar to the detective novels of Agatha Christie, containing as it did many false clues, leading the reader and Tintin in the wrong direction, and creating a masterclass of a farce or comedy of errors.

However, as it was so different to his previous work, it was not as commercially successful as other Tintin stories and never gained the public recognition it truly deserved after it finished in September 1962.

In any case, Hergé was happy with the story and enjoyed working on the books. He was also more relaxed now that the dust had settled in his private life.

By 1964, he was focusing again on the *Tintin* magazine, and he was not happy with what he saw. Hergé found parts of the weekly to be coarse in humour and was generally tired of the publication. As a consequence of this, he and Raymond Leblanc were in an almost constant state of conflict.

Hergé decided the answer was to work closely with the editor-in-chief, currently Marcel Dehaye, Hergé's former secretary, as he wanted to exercise greater control of the cartoonists. He wanted to return to his former role of artistic director, but when he talked to Leblanc about this in July, Leblanc was reluctant, and reminded Hergé of his frequent absences and all the times he had not completed the duties of the role over the past few years.

Hergé replied that he did not have to provide a detailed justification for his decision to resume artistic direction of a magazine that carried the name of the hero he created. He said that he should not have to undergo a cross-examination to return to *Tintin*.

The two men could not agree and eventually lawyers were called upon to settle the dispute. By September, Hergé was determined to either return to his former role as artistic director on the magazine, or he would cancel the agreement with Leblanc. Leblanc held firm until January 1965, when it seemed he would allow Hergé to return to the role, and by February Hergé had an office in the magazine's headquarters. He told the team that he would be at the offices often and that everything published from then on would require his approval.

However, Hergé's heavy-handedness with his staff precipitated many problems. At that time, readers of *Tintin* magazine were asked to vote for their favourite comic strips in the weekly. One of the cartoonists, Dino Attanasio, who drew 'Signor Spaghetti', usually received far fewer votes than the other cartoonists. This year he took matters into his own hands by buying a stack of *Tintin* magazines and voting for his own comic strip.

Eventually finding out about this, Hergé was furious. He formed a tribunal consisting of other artists such as Weinberg and Greg. Together, they decided to suspend Attanasio for three months.

Attanasio's collaborator and text writer was René Goscinny, the author behind the *Asterix* series, which was becoming more and more popular at this point. He promptly resigned from his post, shocked by the treatment of his friend. Greg also left, and Hergé hastily escaped to Sardinia for six weeks with Fanny after he realised what a mess this was becoming.

Greg said he would return if he was made editor-in-chief and was free to modernise the increasingly old-fashioned magazine in an attempt to boost sales. Raymond Leblanc approved the move and on 1 October 1965, when the magazine celebrated its nineteenth year, Marcel Dehaye was replaced by Greg.

Hergé was on good terms with the new editor-in-chief and the magazine was selling well. With 600,000 copies sold each week, it was at its peak. However, Hergé, who had fought so hard to regain his place as artistic director of the weekly, suddenly lost his momentum and did not want to be involved with *Tintin* magazine any more.

However, he set his staff to work on creating a modern version of *The Black Island*, which would appear in the magazine from 1 June to 28 December 1965. The new version would correct any inaccuracies or out-of-date features, with the idea being that the book could then be published in the country in which it had been set, the UK. Bob De Moor even went on a fact-finding mission and visited all the locations in England to make sure the story was as current as possible.

Hergé found his studio system quite constraining by now, as he had to make sure there were enough projects to keep his staff occupied at all times. On staff now was Jacques Martin and Baudouin, both of whom vied for position as Hergé's closest ally. There was also Roger Leloup and Michel Demarets, and the assertive Josette Baujot, who was the only one not afraid to argue with Hergé. And finally, Bob De Moor, a genial type who loved a joke. They would gather for tea at 4 pm sharp every day.

While he was less keen on the work, Hergé loved to take time to look over letters he had received and talk about books, such as those by Jung, with Baudouin. He would spend time with visitors and enjoyed long lunches. He was enjoying his freedom and struggled to concentrate on the comic strips. He also did not appreciate any of his staff trying to rush him. When people approached him with urgent issues, he would tell them that the matter would be much less urgent in a week.

It was at this time that Hergé finally tried his hand at painting. He had felt so constrained by the way his Tintin series had developed, by the need for realism and factual accuracy that had in many ways become a hallmark of the stories, and found that this new form of artistic expression let him break free. But he would still occasionally make notes and sketches for a new Tintin story.

It was an idyllic time for him outside of work, too. He would often take long weekends away with Fanny. When they left for their latest trip to Switzerland, Martin and De Moor, who were tired of waiting for their boss to give them another story to work on, flicked through his notes and sketches and decided to finish a section on their own. They left the piece on his desk and when Hergé returned from his relaxing break to find the work, he was shocked, and exclaimed, 'Good God, the bastards!'

However, even this less than subtle hint from his staff telling him they were bored and were quite capable of taking over the work for him if he so wished, did not spur him on. He did not feel the least bit inspired to start another Tintin story – he was enjoying his free time too much.

By 1966, he considered creating one last Tintin book, but soon dropped the idea, lacking any enthusiasm to return to the comic strip. He would turn to Jacques Martin one day and simply say, 'I hate Tintin'. His staff realised it would take something momentous to truly inspire Hergé to start working again. That soon arrived in the form of a comic that was becoming a serious rival for Tintin – *Asterix*.

The *Asterix* comic strip had started in *Pilote* magazine, which launched in 1959. Created by René Goscinny and Albert Uderzo, it had gained popularity fairly quickly, and by 1966 the eighth book, *Asterix in Britain*, was published, selling an astronomical 600,000 copies. This was a huge number for the time and fuelled interest in the previous volumes, which were then reprinted to feed that demand.

The speed at which Goscinny and Uderzo were producing the books was also impressive – there were two new books each year. The press reported on 'the Asterix phenomenon', and while Hergé was aware of the series, he was unperturbed until he saw the press cuttings Baudouin brought to him one day.

The headlines read 'Tintin is eating the dust kicked up in Asterix's wake' and 'Asterix is now enjoying the success that was formerly Tintin's'. Hergé was apoplectic, retorting, 'Formerly Tintin's! I'll show them "formerly Tintin's!"' And with that, he was back to work.

Hergé and his staff started on *Flight 714* almost immediately, such was his anger at being usurped in the eyes of the press and his fans. *Flight 714 to Sydney* was originally published in English as *Flight 714*, and started in *Tintin* magazine in September 1966. In the story, Tintin becomes involved in a plot to kidnap an eccentric millionaire from a supersonic jet on an Indonesian island, with the title referencing a flight that Tintin manages to miss.

Hergé had always been interested in the paranormal and with *Flight 714 to Sydney*, he wanted to address the question of whether there were other inhabited planets, and also to ask if there were people who knew about them.

He was particularly influenced by Robert Charroux's *The Book of Betrayed Secrets*, which suggested that extra-terrestrials had influenced humanity during the prehistoric period.

Hergé also decided to reintroduce Skut, the Estonian pilot, and Rastapopoulos, both last seen in *The Red Sea Sharks*, as well as bringing new characters into the fold, such as Carreidas, who was based on the French aerospace tycoon, Marcel Dassault.

Hergé would draw the basis of the new series, but then had his assistants complete the backgrounds, detail and colour. In his quest for precision, Hergé copied photos of Etna and Kilauea erupting to depict the volcano.

He also wanted the supersonic Carreidas 160 jet to be as detailed and plausible as the fictional vehicles that had gone before, from Unicorn ships to moon rockets. Hergé was now sixty and he was beginning to suffer from eczema on his drawing hand, so he left the technical jet sketching to his young colleague, Roger Leloup, who was known as a technical artist and aviation expert at Studios Hergé. Leloup had drawn the moon rocket, as well as the de Havilland Mosquito in *The Red Sea Sharks* and, of course, came up with a meticulous design.

The story was well received and showed Hergé to be on top form. Artistically, the comic strip had never looked better, especially the temple and volcanic eruption scenes. However, the adventure was the most far-fetched of the series, with the villains almost becoming farcical parodies of themselves.

Casterman was thrilled to finally have a new Tintin book to market after waiting for so long, and they were keen to make this a real rival to the juggernaut that was *Asterix*. The unfortunate promotional party was usurped by the enormous student protests in the news. However, the book was a huge success, selling 500,000 copies.

But it wasn't good enough for Hergé. *Asterix* was still outselling even the latest Tintin book and sales were rising fast.

Hergé looked to use the medium of film to make Tintin more current, and a version of *Prisoners of the Sun* was released in 1969, with *Tintin and the Lake of Sharks* appearing in 1972, but both failed to capture the essence of the books. Meanwhile, the *Asterix* films were a great success, and Tintin was finding it hard to compete on either paper or the big screen.

Chapter 17

While Hergé was struggling professionally, his personal life was blossoming. He was enjoying life with Fanny and made sure that with this relationship, he set the right foundations from the very beginning by separating work from his personal life, which had been inextricably linked in his marriage with Germaine.

Although he had met Fanny at work, their relationship was different. Hergé appreciated Fanny for her patience, as well as her sense of humour and while he would often bring letters home to talk about, he did not bring the serious side of the business to her. Home was now a much more relaxed and separate entity to the office.

He also made sure he took time to relax, which was something he hadn't done in the early years with Germaine. Hergé previously smoked a great deal, around two packets of cigarettes a day. After he left Germaine, he stopped smoking suddenly and stopped drinking as much, as well. He calmed down in other ways too. Although he had always liked driving fast sports cars, he now chose less flashy models and would even have someone drive him from time to time if he felt it was a wiser option.

Many of his friendships had changed in the aftermath of the split with his wife, with a great number of people siding with Germaine, so his social life changed around this time as well. Hergé was not a party person and hated small talk along with the idea of 'society' gatherings, so he and Fanny would enjoy intimate dinner parties with close friends instead.

He was always a very private person, but as he became more famous, he became even more guarded. He would always have hotel rooms booked under 'Remi' rather than 'Hergé' and it took time before he would fully trust new people.

Hergé loved to spend time with Fanny and they would often escape the city during September to find a quiet spot on Lake Geneva in Switzerland. Other times they would visit the rugged terrain of the Ardennes in south-east Belgium for a more adventurous hiking trip.

With Fanny's influence, Hergé began to try new things. While his holidays were previously confined to nearby European countries, she encouraged him to venture further afield. The first big trip they took was to the United States. Fanny was keen to take full advantage of the holiday to visit a whole host of different cities, such as Chicago, New York, Washington, Las Vegas and Los Angeles. Hergé was not keen and thought it was a crazy plan. However, once the happy couple arrived in the States, he was enchanted with the place and would have extended the trip if they had been able to.

On this trip, Hergé had the opportunity to visit an Indian reservation, fulfilling a long-held ambition and many boyhood dreams, but sadly it did not live up to his expectations.

At this time Hergé finally felt a sense of peace and harmony in his relationships and was happy. He would later say that he had arrived at a clear-headed state quite late in life. He spent his time pursuing his interests and passions, and continued to read the work of Jung, which had helped to free him from the constraints of his Catholic upbringing to some extent.

He was still in contact with some of his old friends, such as Paul Jamin, and would visit Robert Poulet from time to time, occasionally travelling to Paris to see Raymond De Becker.

With the new-found time and clarity of mind, Hergé decided to revisit an old ambition of his – to paint. Rather than spend time fumbling around learning the basics, he contacted a seasoned artist, Louis Van Lint, whom he considered a man 'of rigorous honesty in his judgments', to teach him.

Louis Van Lint was a renowned Belgian painter, known for his abstract artwork. He had been given a prize by the Guggenheim Foundation in 1958, and became a member of the Royal Academy of Belgium in 1960. He gave Hergé private lessons for a year and his protégé created a total of thirty-seven paintings, some with Lint's instruction and some without, but these paintings have never been exhibited.

Hergé asked for opinions on his paintings from a few people close to him, as well as Leo Van Puyvelde, an art historian, and the response to his work was not overly enthusiastic. While his friends thought the pictures were in no way bad, they paled in comparison to the genius of his work on Tintin.

He was disappointed but glad to have tried out painting, and felt it was a rite of passage he needed to go through, but Hergé quickly realised that his efforts were not sufficiently original or interesting enough to keep pursuing. Very quickly he returned to what he felt he did best – comic strips. Hergé made the decision not to exhibit the body of work he had created and left painting behind for good. It was all or nothing for him and he did not want to be an amateur painter or merely a hobbyist.

When people mooted the idea that comic strips were a form of art in 1967, he replied saying that maybe one day someone would be able to ennoble his craft. He felt that a comic strip could be art and said that there was research currently being done on the subject. But he also said that the whole topic made him feel very uncomfortable.

However, after many artists Hergé had admired repeatedly told him how much they loved the Tintin series, his opinion seemed to change ever so slightly, and he started to refer to comic strips as 'a method of total expression', adding that in some ways it was more complete than painting, as comic strips also incorporated a story element.

Fast-forward to 1970, and Hergé started to question whether there was more intelligence, composition and art to be seen in a comic strip such as *Peanuts* than in various collections of splotches that people dared to show at painting exhibitions. He was clearly coming around to the idea that the comic strip was very much an art form and expressed his opinions more robustly than he had before. He added that there were great similarities between painting and the comic strip, especially during the initial stages.

Although he had stopped painting, he still carried an intense interest in the world of contemporary art, being led by one of his long-time friends, Marcel Stal. Stal was a former soldier and friend of Hergé's brother, Paul. After Stal left the army, he opened an art gallery, named Carrefour, situated very close to Studios Hergé, with Hergé funding the first three months' rent for him.

Stal later said that Hergé had wanted him near. Indeed, Hergé loved having his friend so close and would go and visit him every day at 12.05 precisely for a cocktail, usually a 'French', which was a mix of vermouth and gin. Hergé would mingle with the other collectors and loved spending time chatting with them about art. This is how he met Stephane Janssen who became a good friend of his. Janssen had left his wife and children after he came out as gay, and Hergé was amazed by Janssen's courage and found him a fascinating person.

Hergé was enjoying the new influences around him and loved exploring the burgeoning art scene. He enjoyed a wide range of styles, but was particularly interested in Pop Art at this time. He loved Roy Lichtenstein, possibly because he was so famously influenced by the comic book style, but also because Hergé thought he was the cleanest and most graphic of all the American artists of the 1960s, and he proudly displayed Lichtenstein's pictures on his office walls.

It was in the informal salon of the gallery in 1965 that Hergé met Pierre Sterckx, a young art critic. Hergé took advantage of this opportunity and invited Sterckx to visit him at his house once a week to discuss art. It was through these meetings that Hergé learned about the work of Roland Barthes and Claude Levi-Strauss, and he became interested in more conceptual art styles.

Hergé was having a great time exploring the world with Fanny and discovering the art scene. He had little time for *Tintin* magazine, and was no longer interested in this part of his work.

However, Hergé continued to work with his book publisher, Casterman, but was frustrated at their lacklustre attitude to reprinting his books. During the 1960s, the attacks on Hergé's character had continued, partly due to his collaboration during the Occupation, but he was also criticised by those looking back on his earlier books and finding the crude stereotyping offensive. *Tintin in the Congo* was deemed the worst in this respect. Casterman refused to reprint it, although Hergé had repeatedly asked them and had removed some of the most racist passages from the book to pacify the critics.

It wasn't until May 1970 that the publisher gave in and finally reprinted the title. This sparked new interest in the series and Casterman wanted Hergé to make some of his other earlier stories more politically correct so they could reissue versions of those as well.

Hergé was reluctant to give in to his publisher who he said was 'wary of offending the sensibilities of Third World people, and even more so those of their proponents in Paris or Brussels,' but nevertheless, he made significant changes to his stories.

He altered *Land of Black Gold*, taking out the Jewish terrorists and the English occupiers, but later said he had changed the book to make the story clearer and more timeless. He felt the idea of the British occupation of Palestine was too fixed in a certain time, but there could always be a rivalry between two emirs. He denied it was to avoid the dubious politics and insisted it was to make the adventure more understandable and to help the readability.

The task now was to redact points of history that had been a crucial part of his books when first released. When they were first coloured and reissued, references to Belgium were mostly removed to widen their appeal, and now the aim was to remove their context in time.

As Hergé was not producing any new material, he was keen to reprint as many of the older titles as possible. He was even keen to reissue the book he had once found incredibly embarrassing, *Tintin in the Land of the Soviets*.

The style of the drawings in this early book was different to the rest of the series, and difficult to colour in the same way. In 1961, Hergé decided it would be best to publish the story as it was in its original state with a statement from the publisher explaining the context in which it was created.

Casterman was not convinced and lacked enthusiasm for this project. However, collectors were very keen to acquire this book and it wasn't long before pirated editions were released. To counteract this, Studios Hergé printed 500 copies of *Tintin in the Land of the Soviets*, but this only fuelled the fire as even more pirated versions then appeared.

Hergé wanted to produce a legal edition of the book, but Casterman still refused due to the content issues. It was only when Hergé threatened to take the book to a rival publisher that Casterman relented, and published the book within the 'Hergé Archives', along with *Tintin in the Congo* and *Tintin in America*. They added a preface warning the reader of the context of the time and the influences on Hergé as he had created these books.

By 1968 comic strips were beginning to be taken more seriously as an art form. One university student, Pierre Fresnault, even wrote his thesis on Tintin as a study of comic strip art. Hergé was flattered and would exchange long letters with him to help with the project and asked to meet him if he were ever in Belgium. They did eventually meet, and Hergé even sent the student a copy of *Tintin in the Land of the Soviets* as a thank you for his work.

Hergé was a keen correspondent, and would reply to thousands of his young fans. He once said that to not reply to children's letters would be to betray their dreams, and he was keen to stay true to his readers.

Indeed, in 1963, when a young boy called Jacques Langlois sent Hergé a book of drawings in the style of Tintin, Hergé wrote back straight away to tell him that nothing had given him so much pleasure as the young boy's book. Hergé was touched by the boy's efforts and thanked him warmly.

Hergé was an attentive correspondent with children, and although he did not like large-scale autograph sessions and would refuse school visits to the Studios, he often gave access to keen readers and would spend time talking to them. He replied to adults too, from all over the world, and often sent out some of his books and drawings. On occasion he would even loan money to some of these people.

Usually typed out, it is difficult to judge whether these letters were written by Baudouin or Hergé, but Hergé certainly wrote a large proportion of them as he remembered the children he had written to with great clarity. Hergé even met Langlois in 1964 and wrote to him after that, referring back to their meeting. However, the significant number of letters and correspondence increased from the 1950s and Baudouin was of huge assistance with this.

As his fame grew, Hergé was asked more and more often to give interviews, and while he was happy to talk about his work, he was always reluctant to talk about his private life, especially after his split from Germaine.

In June 1970, Hergé's father, Alexis, died at the age of eighty-seven. Hergé felt this loss intensely and went through a more introspective period, examining their relationship.

Soon after, he met Numa Sadoul at the Nice Book Fair, who suggested they conduct a series of interviews with the idea of eventually publishing a book of the results.

Hergé was uncharacteristically keen and they conducted twelve hours of interviews at the Studios and at Hergé's apartment between 20 and 26 October 1971.

For Hergé, giving someone this level of access was unprecedented. Sadoul asked him all kinds of probing questions, which the cartoonist was happy to answer. Hergé even gave Sadoul keys to the Studios, so he could access whatever documents he wanted. He was given free rein to examine the notoriously private Hergé's life.

Sadoul transcribed all the interviews ready for publication and sent them to Hergé for approval, as per their agreement. But Hergé was a perfectionist. He rewrote everything and would go back over what he had already accepted, starting from scratch, refining the ideas and honing the style an extraordinary number of times. It took him three years to send a finished manuscript back to Sadoul, and he was still working furiously on the text just before printing started.

Indeed, Hergé and Baudouin spent a great deal of time going over the interviews and amending various details, but the main changes involved deleting anything related to Fanny, as well as any harsh remarks he had made concerning his staff and comments on his unhappiness over what happened during the Purge.

His book publisher, Casterman, still retained its religious roots and also requested that any negativity towards Catholicism should be removed. Consequently, any allusion to the fact that Hergé struggled with his religion and, in fact, had never felt any religious faith at all was taken out.

After all the changes and edits, the book of interviews was published in 1975. Despite all the editing, there was still a huge amount of new material left in. Hergé addressed all the common criticisms he had faced, such as the issues with his first books, his role during the war and accusations of collaboration, as well as allegations of misogyny within his work. He even talked vaguely about one of his depressive crises from 1959.

More positive subjects were also touched upon, where he discussed significant moments in his life, such as the time he met Abbot Wallez and also the influence of Zhang and Jacobs, but in general he oversimplified many aspects and situations in his life, and it was a sanitised version of the original interviews he had done with Sadoul. He was not yet divorced so no mention of Fanny was made at all, with this major episode in his life completely skipped over.

Although the whole process took an extremely long time and was heavily edited, this was a coup for Sadoul as the famously reticent Hergé had not conducted an interview like this before, and after this experience, Hergé was more open to interviews.

When he was approached by film director Henri Roanne, who asked if a film had been made about the cartoonist, Hergé was keen and suggested that Roanne should make one. Baudouin even followed up soon after to show that Hergé was serious about the project.

The Jewish Roanne was from Austria and had moved to Brussels to escape persecution from the Nazis during the war. The two men with very different backgrounds met and talked a great deal. Roanne specifically wanted to know more of Hergé's attitude during the war. When not being recorded, Hergé said to the director, 'If I had known the extent of the horror, there are drawings I never would have done.' He added after a pause, 'Maybe I made sure I wouldn't know.'

Hergé exerted very little control over the project this time. He gave Roanne access to his archives and left him to finish the film uninterrupted. One result of these probing interviews was that Hergé started to think more about the past and re-examine his experiences and friendships. After talking with Sadoul, Hergé realised how much Zhang had influenced him and his drawing style at that early stage in his life.

Similarly, creating *Tintin in Tibet* had also made him think of Zhang more often, whereas prior to this he had only thought fleetingly of his friend. He vowed to find Zhang. He had no idea where his friend now lived or how to contact him, so he started the search by asking any Chinese people he would happen to meet if they knew Zhang Chong Ren.

Unsurprisingly, this approach did not yield any results. However, in November 1972, Hergé received a letter sent from Taiwan. The letter was from Mr Tsai, who was reissuing the invitation from thirty-five years earlier to visit the country from 'the same government, under the leadership of the same man, and in the name of the same people'.

This had been instigated by a journalist and friend of Hergé's, Dominique de Wespin, who visited Taiwan in 1971 and reminded her contacts of the invitation they had made to Hergé so long ago.

Hergé was keen, but sought advice from Father Neut, who had passed on the original invitation to him. But Father Neut, who was more conscious of the political situation in China and Taiwan at the time, urged him not to accept, telling him that while in 1939 Tchang Kai-Shek had been the leader of the Chinese state, he was no longer in charge. Neut felt that the days of his government on Formosa were numbered, and added that if Hergé were to visit Taiwan, the political situation in that area was so tense it would make it extremely difficult for him to ever visit China.

Undeterred by Father Neut's advice, Hergé accepted the invitation and travelled to Taiwan, but was disappointed with the experience and he was no closer to finding Zhang despite quizzing the people he met on his travels.

A few years later in 1975, Hergé visited Ming's Garden, a Chinese restaurant in Brussels. While there he asked the restaurant owner, Mr Wei, if he knew his old friend. Mr Wei struggled to make out Hergé's pronunciation, but eventually understood. Incredibly, the restauranteur was actually Zhang's godson, but he hadn't heard anything of his godfather for nearly twenty years. He promised to ask his brother, who lived in Shanghai, if he had more details. His brother replied quickly and told him that Zhang also lived in Shanghai, and gave Wei the much sought-after address.

In an extraordinary twist to this tale, the address given to Hergé was the very same address he had been given so many years earlier by his friend, the same one that was in an old address book in his house! From Wei, he learned that Zhang was now a successful artist.

Hergé wrote to his friend on 1 May 1975, exactly forty-one years to the day after their very first meeting, and he was clearly overjoyed to be able to contact his 'dear Zhang' after so many years. He told him how emotional he felt to learn that his friend knew Wei's brother, was living in Shanghai and was now a famous sculptor. He added that when he had been given his friend's address, he felt himself transported back in time to forty years earlier as it was all so familiar to him.

Hergé enthusiastically told him what had happened in his own career and enclosed the two books that had featured Zhang, *The Blue Lotus* and *Tintin in Tibet*. He told him that it had been fifteen years since the last book was published and noted that the book had ended with Tintin finding his Chinese friend Chang again, the same one he had known in *The Blue Lotus*. Hergé felt it was a curious foreshadowing of what was actually happening in reality, and told Zhang that he had never lost hope of finding him.

With great passion, he told his friend how grateful he was for the help he had given him in his early work, but also for helping him to discover so many new things at the time, such as poetry and 'a sense of unity between man and the universe'. Hergé told him that it was thanks to Zhang that his life had taken a new direction, and he wanted to express to him his loyal friendship and sincere gratitude.

Zhang received the letter gratefully, but he was in a dire state. After he had arrived back in Shanghai in 1936, he held a number of shows exhibiting his drawings and sculptures, and also set up the Chongren Studio from which he could teach. He had been a successful sculptor and became the director of the Fine Arts Academy in Shanghai, but the Cultural Revolution had halted this suddenly. He had been forced to destroy his many works of art and attend a 're-education camp', before being sent to work as a street sweeper.

Zhang wrote back to Hergé but could not tell him of the poor situation he was in for fear that government officials would read his letters. He also found it difficult to express himself clearly as he had forgotten much of the French he had learnt and was no longer so fluent in the language.

However, Hergé inferred the details of his friend's situation from speaking to others about the events in China at the time, and they continued to exchange letters. Hergé wanted to travel to China to meet his long-lost friend, but as predicted by Father Neut years earlier, as he had visited Taiwan, it was now incredibly difficult for him to get a Chinese visa.

Gerard Valet, who had co-authored the film *Moi, Tintin* with Henry Roanne, was travelling to China on a work trip and visited Zhang while he was there, with a view to helping him travel back to Belgium, but it would be years before he managed to make this happen.

Chapter 18

Aside from the contact with his old friend, life for Hergé continued as it had before. He was not keen to work, but kept his staff at the Studios busy with small jobs such as postcards and other similar projects. He continued to visit his country house in Ceroux-Mousty every Monday to spend time with Germaine, and the rest of the time he found various ways to distract himself from settling down to create the next instalment of Tintin. He would talk for hours with the art critic, Pierre Sterckx, or spend time with Francois Riviere, a young writer.

Occasionally, he would work on a story that had started life in note form in 1962, called *Tintin et les Bigotudos*, set in San Theodoros, and inspired by events in South America and people such as Fidel Castro and Che Guevara.

This would eventually become *Tintin and the Picaros*, and would be the last complete story that Hergé would make. It began in *Tintin* magazine in September 1975, and the adventure follows Tintin, Snowy, Captain Haddock and Professor Calculus as they travel to the fictional South American nation of San Theodoros to rescue Bianca Castafiore, who had been captured by the government of General Tapioca. Tintin and his team meet their old friend General Alcazar, and become involved in his revolutionary work.

With the help of the group of artists at his Studios, Hergé began work on *Tintin and the Picaros* eight years after completing *Flight 714 to Sydney*. In this new title, the characters change in many ways. Hergé was keen to update Tintin's look, so the adventurer now wore a sheepskin flight jacket, open-faced helmet emblazoned with a CND symbol, and fashionable bell-bottoms rather than his trademark plus-fours. He is also seen practising yoga in another departure for the hero.

Many characters from previous Tintin stories make an appearance, such as Pablo, Ridgewell and the Arumbaya tribe from *The Broken Ear*, as well as Colonel Sponz from *The Calculus Affair*. General Tapioca, who had been mentioned but never seen before, was introduced, and there is a new character, Peggy Alcazar, who was based upon the secretary of a Ku Klux Klan spokesman Hergé had seen in a documentary.

The comic strip ended in the magazine in April 1976, and was published as a book by Casterman later that year, with a launch party held at the Hilton Hotel in Brussels.

However, *Tintin and the Picaros* did not receive a rave reception. Some complained that the story was boring, others criticised the ideology and politics of the book. Neither the critics nor the fans were happy with the lacklustre story they had waited so long for. Despite this, the book sold 1,500,000 copies, but Hergé was upset at the criticism, particularly relating to the politics, and would say that neither he nor Tintin could resolve the problems of the Third World.

Usually laissez-faire in his approach to starting a new book, Hergé was spurred on by the negative feedback and began to prepare the next adventure immediately, which was inspired by a long wait he had had at an airport in Rome in 1973.

He was keen for the next Tintin story to take place entirely inside an airport, as they were geometric hubs with people of all different nationalities passing through. He thought something very funny could be done with this scenario, but he needed to come up with the plot.

Hergé made reams of notes, collating all his ideas, but in trying to include all the characters from previous books and contain them in one space, it had proven to be a very complex tale. By November 1977, he was struggling to finish and wrote to Zhang for advice. He told him all about his problems with his work and said that although he had lots of ideas and themes, he felt that none were quite good enough to form a cohesive narrative.

While he would usually incorporate his current interests into the Tintin stories, he felt that his particular preoccupations at the moment weren't really suitable. Both he and Fanny were deeply interested in Eastern philosophy. Fanny was especially taken with Hinduism, while he was fascinated by Buddhism and Taoism.

Hergé was indeed a deep thinker and would ruminate on subjects for a long time. Relatively pessimistic in his outlook, he was always in search of something. He had thought that Fanny would meet all these needs, but he needed more. He had also thought that painting would be the answer, but it left him wanting.

Art dealer and close friend of Hergé, Marcel Stal later said the cartoonist had a kind of anxiety, which he bore to an astonishing degree. He said the fact that man never attains perfection made Hergé sad and that he always wanted more, he was always seeking something else. Stal thought Hergé didn't have the knack for happiness and didn't know how to experience life like a normal person. There was always a problem, a well of dissatisfaction that affected everything in his life, and fame changed none of this for him. Indeed, he did not revel in the fame he had achieved, and rarely attended events except when forced to by his publisher.

Hergé's private life was still complicated by the fact that he remained married to Germaine but was living with Fanny. While he continued to visit Germaine every Monday, he would occasionally say to friends that when the new divorce law went into effect, he would be the first client.

It was on 28 March 1977 that his separation from Germaine was finally made official with a divorce. Germaine was distraught and deeply hurt at the thought of no longer being his wife. Hergé told Germaine that he still had friendship, affection, and gratitude for her, and would continue to provide for her financially, but this did not lessen the blow.

Just a few weeks after the divorce was finalised, Hergé and Fanny married. They had a small ceremony with just a couple of friends attending as witnesses. Hergé was sixty-nine years old, Fanny was forty-two and they were deeply in love. This ceremony marked a new chapter in their lives together.

Hergé's right-hand-man, Baudouin van den Branden de Reeth had had a stroke in 1974, which was a blow to Hergé – he had relied on him for help professionally and also as a close friend. Hergé hoped Baudouin would get better and return to work, and although he did make a good recovery, he lost the ability to read and write. For a time, he hired Baudouin's wife, Jacqueline, to replace her husband, but this pairing did not work out.

She was eventually replaced by Alain Baran, the son of Hergé's old friend, Dominique de Wespin. Hergé had first met Wespin, who was a great traveller, in 1939 and they had remained close friends. Alain Baran had studied journalism for a while, before embarking on a career as a ballet dancer in 1971. By 1977, he was looking for a new role.

Hergé decided to invite Baran to lunch one day, taking him to La Cravache d'Or, one of the finest restaurants in Brussels. Here, he asked Baran to become his new secretary. Baran was enthusiastic as he greatly admired Hergé, but felt too inexperienced for the role. Hergé was charmed by Baran and, as he had known him since he was a child, watching him grow up, he was certain he had made the right decision.

Although Hergé had made the job sound very straightforward to Baran, when the young man started, he found it anything but easy. Hergé was initially upset with some of his work, but he was persuaded by France Ferrari to give him a second chance and teach him how to fulfil the duties expected of him, and they eventually worked well together.

Tintin's fiftieth anniversary was fast approaching, and Baran was set to work arranging the events to celebrate the occasion. There was a large reception in the prestigious Hotel Carnavalet in Paris, while in Brussels, there was a grand event at the Hilton Hotel. The room was full to the brim with every cartoonist in Belgium coming to celebrate the creator of Tintin. Hergé gave each guest a book rather sarcastically entitled *Fifty Years of Utterly Happy Work*.

Hergé and Tintin received a great deal of media attention that year, and there was even a superb exhibition, entitled 'The Imaginary Museum of Tintin' set in the Palais de Beaux-Arts in Brussels, by Hergé's close friend Pierre Sterckx and Pichel Baudson. The world of Tintin was exhibited with various artefacts that had inspired the stories, and there were even items from the African Museum in Tervuren. In a case of life imitating art, a copy of the Arumbaya fetish was stolen from the exhibition in an incident reminiscent of the events in *The Broken Ear*.

Although Hergé was enjoying the attention and accolades to a degree, it was not an overly happy time for him. In the summer of 1979, he started to feel fatigued. He had had a great number of work events that year, so it was easy to blame the tiredness on overwork.

But by September, doctors investigated further and Hergé was diagnosed with a condition called osteomyelofibrosis, a serious blood disease in which his white blood cells no longer regenerated themselves.

Hergé was devastated – he prized his health and independence above all else. The illness meant he had to have a complete blood transfusion every two weeks. On the face of it, he seemed to take the matter in his stride, often telling people, 'I've refilled my fuel tank,' after he had been to his latest appointment at the hospital. But underneath the bravado, he was struggling.

This was another period in which he would jot down the details of his dreams, but this time they were of a more macabre tone, filled with dark foreboding colours, as opposed to his previous dreams of white. He would dream of friends who had passed away and of sailing in black, threatening water.

He also dreamed of Germaine once again, his guilt from the past few years resurfacing. At one point, he dreamed they were walking in the countryside together. He crossed a stream and asked Germaine to come with him, but she had taken a different path and had sunk into the marshy ground and disappeared. Although the pair were divorced, he still saw Germaine often, but he had not told her of the gravity of his condition.

Hergé now rarely ventured into the Studios. The Editions du Lombard company which made *Tintin* magazine were using Tintin's image for a whole host of advertising projects, and Hergé was too tired to battle with them. He left the day-to-day running of his business to Alain Baran and came to rely on the young man, whom he greatly appreciated. He would often tell him that if he had had a son, he would have loved for that son to be like Baran.

Baran had never known his father and doted on Hergé. Rumours circulated that the young man was actually Hergé's biological son, but there is no proof of this.

By 1981 Baran had been given the role of administrative director of the Studios – a prestigious title and job, showing the trust Hergé placed in him to run matters in his more and more frequent absence. Baran rose to the challenge and was keen to take the reins firmly in hand, and stop Editions du Lombard using Hergé's images for any and every unsuitable advertising campaign.

Hergé left his protégé to handle the issue. He occasionally thought about Tintin, and would look at the notes he had made years earlier on the idea of an adventure set in an airport. This had evolved into a story centred around the art industry, and the airport setting had been dropped. After reading a biography on the forger Fernand Legros, whom Hergé found utterly captivating, he started jotting down ideas for a story about fakery, which would become *Tintin and Alph-Art*.

When he wasn't tinkering with the new story, he spent time learning more on a subject he was passionate about – philosophy. A long-time fan of eastern philosophy, and of the Tao in particular after meeting Zhang, he became interested in the work of Jean Charon, who wrote *The Unknown Mind* and *The Eternal World of Eons*.

Charon was a French nuclear physicist, philosopher and writer who believed in the idea of a form of 'thinking electrons' which implied there was a version of the eternal life. Hergé, who had always been attracted to the idea that there is more out there than we are aware of, and also currently seriously ill, was fascinated by Charon's ideas, and even arranged to meet up with him in Brussels. Hergé and Charon chatted for a long time on the subject and enjoyed each other's company a great deal.

In this period, Hergé often thought of Zhang and they continued to exchange letters. A journalist, Gerard Valet, had been trying to organise a visit back to Brussels for Zhang, but it had proven to be an extremely challenging project, and negotiations with the authorities in China had been ongoing for years. Valet had wanted to bring Zhang over to Belgium in time for the fiftieth anniversary of Tintin, but this had been impossible.

However, two years later, Valet finally managed to arrange for Zhang to travel to Brussels, and he arrived at the airport on 18 March 1981 to an overwhelming welcome from Hergé and a crowd of reporters. Zhang was shocked to be greeted with such fanfare, but he was a central part of the Hergé legend and treated as a star. As the two men embraced after such a long hiatus, the moment had a touching poignancy.

Valet had organised a press conference for Hergé and Zhang, as well as a welcome party, attended by the two men, the press, Hergé's friends and even Father Léon Gosset, who had introduced Hergé to Zhang.

Zhang's extremely long-awaited return seemed to be the perfect end to this tale. It was life imitating art and brought the story of their friendship full circle.

Behind closed doors, however, it was not such an idyllic situation. Hergé had idealised the man he met so long ago, the person who had had such an influence over his life and the path he had taken, but when they reunited, Hergé found the real Zhang bitter and intrusive, and altogether less cordial than expected. They struggled to find the common ground that had once united them and made them so close. Hergé also found the media event too much to deal with in his current state, and hosting Zhang in his house in Dieweg completely overwhelmed him.

Zhang stayed with Hergé and Fanny for a number of weeks, which was altogether too long for Hergé's liking, before returning to China, but the two men remained on good terms.

Chapter 19

By September 1981, Hergé's health had deteriorated even further. He wanted to travel to the Hotel Eden Roc d'Ascona on Lake Maggiore in Switzerland, so his doctor arranged for another hospital to take over his care while he was away from home, as he still needed to have a blood transfusion every two weeks.

Hergé wrote to Zhang while he was away to say that although his health hadn't improved, he felt a great deal better in Switzerland, as the climate at Lake Maggiore was very soothing. While he was there, he felt much less tired, and he was able to swim and go for short walks without feeling too out of breath.

However, shortly after this, Hergé was struck down with double pneumonia and he swiftly returned to Brussels for treatment. He continued to follow his doctor's advice to the letter, and had regular blood transfusions.

The following year he visited the same hotel in Switzerland again for another relaxing holiday, which he mainly spent reclining by the pool. On 5 June 1982, he sent a card to his great friend, the art critic Pierre Sterckx. He told him there was no visiting churches or famous sites this time, just reading for both him and Fanny. While he was working his way through the tomes of the Tao again, Fanny had plunged back into Dickens, which he thought was marvellous.

Hergé tried to stay upbeat and Fanny supported him throughout his illness. He would seem to improve for weeks on end, but then go through weeks of pain. After consulting the doctors, they advised changing to weekly blood transfusions instead, which helped him for a while. With Fanny nearby he continued to enjoy life as much as possible.

Although Hergé suffered from debilitating fatigue, he did not give up and was still hopeful that he would make a full recovery. He threw all his energy into finding a cure, and consulted a range of experts from various fields of Western medicine, as well as traditional Chinese practitioners that Zhang had suggested may be of help. Some specialists advised that even if the illness could not be cured, he might still have a few years ahead of him.

However, this was not to be. His health deteriorated very suddenly. With the frequent blood transfusions he was having, many of those closest to him worried that he was at risk of contracting AIDS, as the illness was not easy to detect at that time.

By 1983, Hergé was in very poor health and on 25 February, he went into cardiac arrest. He was taken to the intensive care centre at the Saint-Luc clinic in Brussels, where he lay in a coma, covered in tubes, with Fanny at his side.

Despite the best efforts of doctors at the hospital, Hergé passed away just a few days later on 3 March 1983. Fanny's last words to her beloved husband were, 'Be free!'

Glowing tributes followed in the days afterwards. The daily French newspaper, *Liberation*, released a special edition illustrated beautifully with images from the Tintin adventures. *Le Soir*, which had not been entirely positive regarding Hergé since the war, celebrated his life and achievements for a whole week.

There was a rush on the bookshops with people desperately trying to complete their Tintin collections, for fear that they would go out of print, and the Hergéan style with the 'ligne claire' or 'clear line' became fashionable again with the new generation of cartoonists for a while.

Fanny and Hergé had had such a close relationship, and she was struggling to come to terms with her grief, but she also faced what seemed like an insurmountable number of duties. Hergé had written his will a few months before he passed away and it consisted simply of one line: 'I make my wife Fanny my sole legatee'.

Although they had met at work, Fanny had left soon after and she had not been involved in Hergé's business at all, rarely even visiting the Studios. Now, she was faced with making all the decisions regarding the Studios and Tintin. Hergé's secretary, Alain Baran, who had been particularly supportive to Fanny as Hergé's health had deteriorated, stepped in to advise and help her with the ever-growing mountain of files she needed to organise. Fanny would have preferred to stay away from business matters, but Baran encouraged her to take charge.

While there was no detailed will, Hergé had made it very clear that he did not want others to continue to produce *The Adventures of Tintin*, feeling that he was the only one who could bring his characters to life – that it was a 'personal oeuvre' and not simply a business.

The staff at the Studios knew there would be no new books, but Bob De Moor was keen to finish *Tintin and Alph-Art*, which he had been working on with Hergé.

Fanny gave De Moor the files that Hergé had created for what would have been his last book, but there was not a great deal of material, and although he worked on the story for a while, Fanny eventually decided to stop production. However, the level of attention given to the mysterious last book was such that she felt obliged to publish the material Hergé had left, and said at a press conference that the work was printed as its author left it, in the original form of forty-two pages of sketches, annotations and texts.

The next issue to address was the running of Studios Hergé. Without Hergé did the Studios have a future? There could be no new projects and Baran felt the Studios had not worked well in many years. The staff had mainly been working on fairly average adverts for a long time, alongside an attempt to make *Quick and Flupke* into a cartoon, which had not been a success.

By November 1986, everyone knew the Studios' time was up. *Tintin and Alph-Art* had just been published with great success, and a few weeks later, Fanny released a statement, announcing the closure of the Studios and the end of an era. She said:

> *'For more than thirty years, the activities of the public company Studios Hergé has been fundamentally connected to the creation of my husband's work. Hergé did not wish for new books to be produced after his death. The publication of the last, unfinished adventure, Tintin and Alph-Art, was an illustration of this; the consequence being that Studios Hergé has lost its principal reason for existing.'*

However, there still needed to be a body that would be able to deal with the canon of work that Hergé had produced, so Fanny created the Hergé Foundation. With the help of Baran, Fanny took charge of licensing issues, too. Hergé had generally left this aspect of work to his staff, and there had been a proliferation of poor adverts and products. The aim now was to ensure Hergé's work was only used for high-quality products, and that no more drawings would be made. The new focus on premium items would be as much for adult collectors as for children.

Tintin magazine was still in production, but bore no resemblance to the original version, and did not feature any of Hergé's characters. The sales fell and Raymond Leblanc sold the company. The magazine finally closed in 1988.

Alain Baran decided to start a new magazine, entitled *Tintin Reporter*, but it was old-fashioned and did not appeal to the children of the day – it was a flop.

However, there were other, more exciting avenues to explore. In the last few months of Hergé's life, in November 1982, Steven Spielberg had contacted him asking for the rights to an adaptation of *The Adventures of Tintin*.

Hergé was thrilled and was keen to give Spielberg free rein to make the project. Although he had once hoped that Walt Disney would make an animated film from the Tintin adventures, he had always preferred the idea of using real actors, saying that was how he saw his characters: 'My Tintin is alive. So is my Captain Haddock. But these films would have to be made with quality and a budget equal to a James Bond film.'

Unfortunately, Hergé never got to see his work receive the big-screen treatment. After Hergé's death, Spielberg flew to Brussels to meet Fanny and Baran, who showed the film director the original panels of work and described what they wanted in the film. Spielberg was captivated by the work and promised to keep to the original tone as much as possible.

Despite a very positive meeting, the details of the contract proved difficult to negotiate as the film company wanted to take control of all matters concerning Tintin, while Baran and Fanny wanted to keep the rights to the original drawn images.

Spielberg was not happy with the scripts he had received and changed his role in the project to that of a producer, and looked for a European director instead. He considered Francois Truffaut and others, before deciding on Roman Polanski, who had long harboured an ambition to make a Tintin film. However, due to the lack of a viable script, in 1987, Spielberg decided not to extend his option on the rights to Tintin.

Although the film was not to be at this time, in 1989, a company called Canal Plus started to produce cartoons for television based on the Tintin stories, with the approval of Fanny and Baran. These were more successful than the previous cartoon versions and were broadcast from 1991 to 1995, causing a significant spike in book sales at the time.

Without any new material being produced, it would be natural to expect the work of Hergé to be easily forgotten, lost in the annals of time. But every year there are exhibitions, books and documentaries about the boy reporter and his creator. There are shops devoted entirely to Hergé's work.

Indeed, on 1 June 2006, the Dalai Lama gave the International Campaign for Tibet's Light of Truth Award to the Hergé Foundation, in recognition of *Tintin in Tibet*. Fanny accepted the award on behalf of the foundation, saying, 'We never thought that this story of friendship would have a resonance more than 40 years later.'

To provide a lasting monument to his work, on 22 May 2009, the Hergé Foundation opened the Hergé Museum outside Brussels in Louvain-la-Neuve. Set in a rather spectacular modernist building designed by the architect Christian de Portzamparc, it is a perfect tribute to Hergé's life and art, displaying collections of photographs, original plates and other documents which tell his extraordinary story.

And in terms of fulfilling one of Hergé's long-held ambitions, Steven Spielberg picked up a new option to make three feature films based on *The Adventures of Tintin*. In 2011, a collaboration between two titans of film, Spielberg and Peter Jackson, of *The Lord of the Rings* fame, resulted in the first Tintin film reaching the big screen.

The Adventures of Tintin: The Secret of the Unicorn was a 3D computer-animated action-adventure film inspired by three of the Tintin books, including *The Crab with the Golden Claws*, *The Secret of the Unicorn* and *Red Rackham's Treasure*. A huge success, it grossed over $373 million and was well received by critics. A sequel has been discussed for many years, but is still in the pipeline.

There have been more than 250 million books sold, Tintin has been translated into over 110 languages and a museum houses the story of Tintin and Hergé's life – few comic strip artists achieve so much.

But what was the secret of his success? The combination of Hergé's famous 'clear line' style, the fast-paced action and the underlying Boy Scout humour mixed with social commentary was a powerful cocktail. But what really set Hergé's series apart from any other were the characters. From Tintin to the Thompson twins, Haddock to Calculus, Castafiore to Wagg, the sheer number and range of colourful characters that pop up in different stories meant that Hergé created his own Tintin universe in a similar way to his own hero, Balzac.

The characters are deceptively simple, memorable and above all relatable. Anyone could be the simple Boy Scout reporter. He didn't need weapons or training, just curiosity and his sidekick, Snowy. The lack of a family or a history meant that anyone in the world could relate to Tintin, and see themselves foiling criminal networks and capturing hard-bitten gangsters.

Although Tintin caused Hergé so much anguish and turmoil over the years, the reporter-turned-explorer has become one of the greatest comic characters of all time and has brought happiness to millions of children and adults alike.

Bibliography

Assouline, Pierre, *Hergé: The Man Who Created Tintin* (Oxford University Press, USA, 2011)

Calamur, Krishnadev, *Coming to Terms With Tintin* (The Atlantic, 2016)

Farr, Michael, *The Adventures of Hergé: Creator of Tintin* (Last Gasp, 2008)

Farr, Michael, *Tintin: The Complete Companion* (Egmont, UK, 2011)

Hergé, *Cigars of the Pharaoh* (Egmont, UK, 2012)

Hergé, *Destination Moon* (Egmont, UK, 2012)

Hergé, *Explorers on the Moon* (Egmont, UK, 2012)

Hergé, *Flight 714 to Sydney* (Egmont, UK, 2011)

Hergé, *King Ottokar's Sceptre* (Egmont, UK, 2010)

Hergé, *Land of Black Gold* (Methuen Children's Books, UK, 1987)

Hergé, *Prisoners of the Sun* (Methuen Children's Books, UK, 1987)

Hergé, *Red Rackham's Treasure* (Methuen Children's Books, UK, 1988)

Hergé, *The Black Island* (Methuen Children's Books, UK, 1988)

Hergé, *The Blue Lotus* (Methuen Children's Books, UK, 1989)

Hergé, *The Broken Ear* (Mandarin Paperbacks, UK, 1989)

Hergé, *The Calculus Affair* (Egmont, UK, 2012)

Hergé, *The Castafiore Emerald* (Egmont, UK, 2012)

Hergé, *The Crab with the Golden Claws* (Egmont, UK, 2012)

Hergé, *The Red Sea Sharks* (Egmont, UK, 2012)

Hergé, *The Secret of the Unicorn* (Methuen Children's Books, UK, 1983)

Hergé, *The Seven Crystal Balls* (Methuen Children's Books, UK, 1982)

Hergé, *The Shooting Star* (Methuen Children's Books, UK, 1987)

Hergé, *Tintin and Alph-Art* (Egmont, UK, 2004)

Hergé, *Tintin and the Picaros* (Egmont, UK, 2012)

Hergé, *Tintin in America* (Egmont, UK, 2012)

Hergé, *Tintin in the Congo* (Casterman, 2016)

Hergé, *Tintin in the Land of the Soviets* (Egmont, UK, 2014)

Hergé, *Tintin in Tibet* (Egmont, UK, 2012)

Judah, Tim, *Tintin in the Dock* (The Guardian, 1999)

Kuper, Simon, *Tintin and the War* (Financial Times, 2011)

McGrath, Charles, *An Innocent in America* (The New York Times, 2012)

Peeters, Benoît, *Hergé, Son of Tintin* (The Johns Hopkins University Press, 2012)

Sadoul, Numa, *Entretiens Avec Hergé* (Casterman, 1983)

Sadoul, Numa, *Tintin et Moi* (Casterman, 1975)

Sterckx, Pierre, *Tintin: Hergé's Masterpiece* (Rizzoli International Publications, 2015)

Thompson, Harry, *Tintin – Hergé & His Creation* (Sceptre, 1992)

Index